GUIDEBOOK
FOR
DIRECTORS
OF
NONPROFIT
CORPORATIONS

GEORGE W. OVERTON, EDITOR

PREPARED BY

THE LEGAL GUIDEBOOK
FOR DIRECTORS SUBCOMMITTEE

NONPROFIT CORPORATIONS
COMMITTEE

SECTION OF BUSINESS LAW
AMERICAN BAR ASSOCIATION

The materials contained herein represent the opinions of the authors and editors and should not be construed to be the action of the American Bar Association or the Section of Business Law unless adopted pursuant to the bylaws of the Association.

Nothing contained in this book is to be considered as the rendering of legal advice for specific cases, and readers are responsible for obtaining such advice from their own legal counsel. This book is intended for educational and informational purposes only.

Library of Congress Catalog Card Number 93-71955
ISBN 0-89707-892-6

Discounts are available for books ordered in bulk. Special consideration is given to state and local bars, CLE programs, and other bar-related organizations. Inquire at Book Development & Marketing, American Bar Association, 750 North Lake Shore Drive, Chicago, Illinois 60611

01 00 99 98 97   5 4 3 2 1

GUIDEBOOK FOR DIRECTORS OF NONPROFIT CORPORATIONS

TABLE OF CONTENTS

PREFACE

This *Guidebook for Directors of Nonprofit Corporations* has been prepared by a subcommittee of the Committee on Nonprofit Corporations of the Business Law Section of the American Bar Association. The purpose of the *Guidebook* is to assist the director of a nonprofit corporation in performing his or her duties. Primarily designed for the lay reader, the *Guidebook* provides a description of general legal principles as they apply to nonprofit corporations and also, on a more practical level, offers what we hope will be useful suggestions and procedures for both the individual director and the corporation which he or she serves.

Although the *Guidebook* is a product of the collaborative effort of a number of lawyers serving on the Legal Guidebook for Directors Subcommittee of the Nonprofit Corporations Committee, assisted by Lauren McNulty (who prepared the chapter on taxation), the principal author is George W. Overton of Chicago, Illinois. George has worked tirelessly to mold the individual efforts into what we all hope will be a useful reference book for directors of the thousands of nonprofit corporations in the United States, from the smallest corporation, operating principally at a local or even neighborhood level, to the largest nonprofit corporation having operations which extend not only across this country but internationally as well.

The Subcommittee is currently working on a supplement to this *Guidebook* which will address specific issues that are pertinent to the operations of many nonprofit corporations, including, for example, antitrust considerations, employee benefit and other labor related issues, financing and securities law issues, and corporation reorganization and bankruptcy issues.

In general, the *Guidebook* addresses general legal principles and broad areas of concern and is not intended to be a source of legal advice or solutions to particular problems. Directors of nonprofit corporations and others charged with responsibility for managing nonprofit corporations are urged to seek advice on both general and particular matters from their corporation's legal advisors and, as appropriate, their own legal counsel.

WILLIAM A. HUMENUK
Co-Chair, Subcommittee
on the Guidebook

A LETTER TO THE READER

The *Guidebook* which follows will speak for itself: but those of us who put it together wish to tell the reader what we did and did not do, and what we hope you are doing or going to do.

We hoped to encourage you (not frighten you!) to continue service as a nonprofit director or to begin such service if you haven't done so yet. Whether you are yet on a board, or about to join one, you come at a time of new tasks dawning: nonprofit corporations have always played a large role in American life; they play a bigger role today than most people realize; and we believe that in the closing years of this century, they will have new loads of unsolved problems thrust at them. Our country needs you and counts on you, all of you, on small boards or large.

We don't purport to give you more than the most rudimentary legal advice; we are giving you more an agenda of things to think about than a set of answers. And, as our drafts grew larger and larger, space requirements dictated the omission of much material. We strongly urge that you read our Introduction, as a guide to what is to be accomplished.

We were further faced with a constant need for balance. If we wrote about boards as they are right now (February 1993) our work would be out of date by the time you saw it; furthermore we would appear to ratify or accept complacently much that is loose or haphazard. If we wrote about what boards may be expected to do in 1998, we would be taking a guess as to the future, and you might think this both loose and arrogant. We hope we have succeeded in making you conscious of the issues to which boards are exposed today, and in suggesting things to think about as the future flings its challenges at us all.

A great university president once said that he looked for three things in a nonprofit director "wealth, wisdom, and work—never settle for less than two." We hope to add to your wisdom by this little handbook: we want to make your work more effective; as for wealth, we can't do much for you. But if all who care for the nonprofits which they direct are wiser and dedicated, there will be wealth, in many forms, for all.

Let us know what you think!

GEORGE W. OVERTON
for the Drafting Subcommittee

INTRODUCTION

A. Why We Wrote This Guidebook

This Guidebook was prepared to aid the director of a nonprofit corporation in performing his or her duties.[1] We write for anyone presently serving as such a director, as well as anyone contemplating such service.

There are a wide variety of nonprofit corporations: trade associations, art museums, health care providers, social clubs, foundations and homeowner associations, just to name a few, and we write for the directors of all of them. These separate types of organizations have many things in common and their directors can benefit from the same advice. From a legal standpoint all these corporations are more alike than different. In most states, nonprofit corporations are formed and maintained pursuant to a single statute; each one has a single board of directors which has the power, conferred by statute, to direct its operations. Nearly all nonprofit organizations are subject to one of a small number of related sections of the Internal Revenue Code. In describing the positive and negative obligations of the directors, anyone advising the director must draw on a single body of law, largely developed for the business corporation.

A wide range of leaders in the political, philanthropic and scholarly world, predict an increasing role and responsibility for the nonprofit sector. We share in this prediction, and we seek to strengthen this response to our nation's needs. The conduct of all nonprofit boards and their capacity to shoulder increasing burdens are of national concern.

In many areas we advocate a formality and regularity in board procedures beyond what is generally observed even in well-managed corporations of long standing. If we do so, it is because we seek to strengthen the corporations for whose directors we write. Nothing we suggest is here for ornament or ceremony.

It may be felt that we urge methods appropriate for large entities but unnecessary in the small local organization; however, nothing we discuss is irrelevant to any nonprofit board, although an organization's response to a need may vary with the size and nature of the operation.

We believe that many readers will share the foregoing concerns and wish to make their corporations sturdier and more effective.

We write for all of you.

INTRODUCTION

B. Our Subject and Some Definitions

A nonprofit corporation is an artificial creation of a government—usually a state—which issued the certificate of incorporation. Corporations do not exist simply by mutual agreement of members or directors but come into being only by a specific act of a state or the federal government and are kept in existence only by compliance with the regular requirements of that government.

As part of the creation of the corporation, the articles of incorporation are filed with the government. These articles are often referred to as a "Charter" or "Constitution." We shall use "articles of incorporation" herein.

Similarly the detailed rules of governance of the corporation, as adopted by it, are usually referred to as the "Bylaws" but sometimes are labelled with other names, such as "standing rules." We shall use "bylaws" herein.

Every nonprofit corporation statute provides for a board of directors; but, in a given corporation, the name of this body varies with the history, tradition—and whim—of the organization involved. It may be called a "Board of Trustees," a "Board of Overseers," a "Governing Committee," or any one of a dozen other names. We shall refer to it as a "board of directors" and to its members as "directors."[2] Throughout this Guidebook, the term "director" is used to denote a member of the board of directors of a nonprofit corporation. Any other type of "director" will be qualified in the text.

We face a similar confusion in the titles of officers. In nonprofit corporations, the term "president" often describes someone who would be called "chairman of the board" in a business corporation; in other organizations the word denotes the paid chief executive officer. We shall use "chair" for the person who presides over the board of directors, and "chief executive" for the principal executive officer of the corporation, who may be called "executive director," "president," or hold some other title. Again, it is possible for a director to be also the chair or chief executive, or to occupy both positions.

In the nonprofit world, "member" may denote a person or entity with voting rights as extensive, or perhaps more extensive, than those of a stockholder of a business corporation; it may be simply a cosmetic term used by a charitable corporation to express appreciation to its donors; or the corporation may have no members at all. We shall refer to "member" only where the word means a person or entity with voting or other significant rights.

In general, we shall conform our terminology to that of the ABA's Revised Model Nonprofit Corporation Act (the "Model Act").[3] We shall refer in this Guidebook to the three classifications of nonprofit corporations set forth in the Model Act:

INTRODUCTION

- "Public benefit corporations," which operate for public or charitable purposes;

- "Mutual benefit corporations," which operate for the benefit of their members; and

- "Religious corporations," which operate to advance or maintain the religion motivating their members or directors.

The reader will note that these definitions do not neatly and precisely divide the universe: What is a hospital which is organized and operated by an order of nuns as a witness to their faith? Or note a trade association—generally a prototype mutual benefit corporation—which publishes standards and instructions to protect worker safety: in doing so does it become a public benefit entity? Nonetheless, the three classifications will aid us in describing the functions of directors in differing contexts.

This Guidebook deals only with nonprofit entities which are organized as corporations. Other nonprofit entities, such as unincorporated associations, charitable trusts or labor unions, are outside the scope of this effort.

C. The Nature Of Our Advice

In advising the director, we seek to answer two principal questions:

- What does the law require?

- What is good corporate practice, as shaped by the needs of the particular corporation involved and the practical limitations of the director's service?

Neither of these questions has a simple answer. Much of the law concerning a director's responsibility is derived from practices in business corporations where the accountability of a director may differ from that arising in a nonprofit context. What constitutes good corporate practice will also vary with the nature and resources of the corporation, its purposes and the nature of its exposures. The practical opportunities available to the director are further shaped by the needs and resources of each corporation involved. Nonetheless there is significant advice which we can give to all directors.

INTRODUCTION

1.   The law's commands

In writing for directors we must first, as lawyers, alert our readers to the commands and prohibitions imposed by the law. All legal systems necessarily deal with <u>minimum</u> requirements of behavior: "You must do <u>at least</u> X" or "<u>No matter what the circumstances,</u> you must not do Y." As lawyers, we shall outline or refer to the major commands: the director <u>must</u> do thus and so; he or she <u>must not</u> do this and that. We shall phrase this part of our advice with the imperative verbs such as <u>must, must not, shall, shall not, is required to,</u> and the like.

Our statements of the law's commands is sometimes a summary of a specific statute or regulation—e.g., the Internal Revenue Code and the related regulations—and sometimes a reference to the body of judge-made law concerning corporations. We shall use the Model Act as the prototype or presumptive guide to issues of statutory corporate law.

2.   Good corporate practice

Equally important, however, is our advice—which we also give as lawyers—outlining what a director <u>should, is expected to, should not,</u> or <u>may</u> do.

What a director <u>should</u> do reflects: (a) policies lying behind the legal requirements; and (b) general standards of corporate management evolved from the experience of both business and nonprofit corporations.

In writing about good corporate practice, we are describing in part what a director is presently generally expected to do; in part, what we believe will probably be expected in the near future; and in part, what we think the dedicated director will want to see from his or her fellow directors, and hence from him or herself.

3.   The practical limitations of the director's service, and the corporation's needs

The most important practical limitation of a director's service is time. Each individual director should determine how much time she or he can devote to the corporation's affairs; and each board of directors should organize its affairs on a shared assumption as to the time all directors can give.

In many of the areas examined in this Guidebook, we can offer no ready-made answer to a specific conflict of needs and resources; but throughout, we will seek to make the director <u>conscious</u> of the difficulty and urge that a specific compromise be <u>created</u>. We shall further repeat—frequently—that these decisions will have to be reviewed periodically:

INTRODUCTION

the corporation will not, and should not, stand still; neither will the environment which surrounds it.

D. The Organization of This Guidebook

We have divided our work as follows:

Chapters I through V, we treat matters which are of concern to all directors of all corporations: how a board works, the functions of committees, the roles of directors and staff, and the director's risk and insurance protection.

In Chapter VI, on Taxation, we survey a concern for all nonprofit corporations and their directors.

In Chapters VII and VIII we suggest standards and procedures for the use of volunteers, advisory boards, director information and orientation.

At the end of each Chapter, the reader will find questions which, we suggest, the individual director should review concerning his or her role on the board of directors. We then follow with a checklist which each corporation may wish to review in light of its needs.

The appendices are self-explanatory.

ENDNOTES

1. (p. 1) This Guidebook is the work of the Committee on Nonprofit Corporations of the Business Law Section of the American Bar Association ("ABA").

2. (p. 2) The special obligations of nonprofit directors who are, under the laws of some states, considered "trustees" and thus subject to duties going beyond those generally applicable to nonprofit directors, is an area which space does not permit us to summarize. In general it is a problem only for directors of corporations or foundations holding (or seeking) assets to be held for charitable purposes. We treat some of the issues thus raised in Chapter I, and Chapter III C, infra. In various jurisdictions, some decisional law, some commentary, and the asserted policies of some regulatory agencies use the term "trustee" as generally synonymous with "fiduciary." The applicable law and its literature is notably obscure. See Olson & Hatch, Director and Officer Liability (1991) ¶ 11.02[1][b]. The Model Act (see below) specifically rejects the trust law standard for the conduct of nonprofit directors. Model Act § 8.30(e).

3. (p. 2) The Revised Model Nonprofit Corporation Act was published by the Business Law Section of the American Bar Association in 1987. We point out that the nonprofit corporation statute of the particular government which created any subject corporation may differ from the Model Act. The reader should, when faced with a specific problem, examine the particular statute governing the corporation in question.

I

THE CORPORATION AND ITS DIRECTORS:
WHAT THEY DO, HOW THEY DO IT, AND FOR WHOM

A. The Zoology Of The Corporate World

1. A director should first understand how corporations are structured.

Anyone serving as a director of a corporation must be aware of what a director is—and isn't. As a body, a board of directors has considerable powers. In most corporations the board plays a substantial part in the beginning or end of any corporate activity, and the board appoints or removes corporate agents, executives and officers.

In contrast, an individual director, acting alone, has almost no power: rather each director exerts her or his power as one participating element in the board of directors.[1] However, the individual director is still legally accountable for corporate actions in certain circumstances and has legally protected rights and duties to participate in the board's decisions and all information related thereto.[2]

The board's powers are exercised for the benefit of others: in a business corporation, primarily for the stockholders; in a nonprofit corporation, for a variety of parties whom we will describe; but the board, and the directors who serve on it, are always judged in terms of their actions on behalf of others.

The corporate structure contemplates that corporate actions, as determined by the board, will be carried out by officers, employees and agents—persons chosen, directly or indirectly, by the board of directors. Often a person serving as a director may also wear another hat, such as that of an officer or agent, but corporate theory assumes that neither the board itself nor any individual director, acting solely as a director, carries out day to day activities.

In many nonprofit corporations there are members, who may be the individuals or entities choosing the directors and who, in some nonprofit corporations, have more extensive powers.[3]

Any corporate director relates to three parties or interests:

> The constituency which elects or appoints him or her;

> The constituency of service—that is, the something or somebody the corporation must serve; and

> The constituency of accountability—the parties who may question the acts or omissions of the board or the individual director.

I THE CORPORATION AND ITS DIRECTORS: WHAT THEY DO, HOW THEY DO IT, AND FOR WHOM

In a business corporation, the foregoing three interests are, for most purposes, identical: the director is elected by the stockholders; her or his primary function is to advance their wealth; and it is the stockholders, in most instances, who may call the director to account.

In the nonprofit world, no such simple answers are available. The persons or entities electing or appointing the nonprofit director, the interests to be served by him or her and those who may call the director to account can be, and often are, separate parties.

2.   <u>**A director should know who selected him or her.**</u>

As to the director's election, selection or appointment, nonprofit corporations can be classified into three groups:

> First, membership corporations, including, for practical purposes, all mutual benefit corporations, elect directors somewhat as the stockholders elect a business corporation director. Usually the members, at an annual meeting, are presented with a slate of candidates for election or re-election; each member has one vote; and the candidate or candidates having the most votes win. This process generally describes those public benefit and religious corporations which have a voting membership of individuals. The same basic structure is used where the members are institutions or even one single person or entity; thus a hospital may create a subsidiary nonprofit corporation for a particular purpose, with the hospital corporation as the sole voting member electing the subsidiary's directors.

> Second, many public benefit and religious corporations have self-perpetuating boards of directors, where the existing board elects—or re-elects—the persons who serve as directors.

> Third, a director may be appointed by another organization or an officer thereof; or she or he may serve ex officio, as described below.

I THE CORPORATION AND ITS DIRECTORS: WHAT THEY DO, HOW THEY DO IT, AND FOR WHOM

3.   Special Categories of Directors

Frequently a nonprofit board will describe some person as an "honorary," "life," "emeritus" or "ex officio" director. These designations often cause confusion.

An "honorary" or "emeritus" director is, almost by definition, not a true director. If a board wishes to recognize some one—usually a longtime member of the board—as deserving of special respect, but to be relieved of regular duties as a board member, no legal problems exist, with three exceptions:

> First, a director, in order to vote, must be elected or appointed in the manner set forth in the bylaws or other corporate documents and applicable law for the designation of voting directors, not by an ad hoc resolution of the board.

> Second, although a board may at any time invite to attend any meeting any person, including "honorary" or "emeritus" directors, their presence may not be counted for a necessary quorum, and such a person may not vote, even if she or he is allowed to participate in discussion at the meeting; the invitation itself confers no voting rights.

> Third, the board, in consulting legal counsel concerning matters which the corporation may wish to consider in confidence, must realize that the presence at a meeting of a non-director, or his or her receipt of confidential documents, may destroy the attorney-client privilege—the corporation's right to communicate with counsel while keeping that communication secret even in court.

"Life" directors occupy much the same position as honorary directors and are subject to the same admonitions set forth above. If a corporation intends to create one or more positions of full voting directorship with a lifetime term, the board should examine the applicable nonprofit corporation statute—many will not permit it. The bylaws then must clearly define the status of such a director.

"Ex officio" directors present more complex problems. To begin with, the words convey two somewhat inconsistent meanings: in one construction, an ex officio director is someone who, by holding some office or position (inside or outside the corporation), becomes entitled to attend meetings and participate therein. The corporate documents should define whether such an ex officio director has a vote. For example, a hospital may designate whomever is chief of the medical staff as an "ex officio director," to serve as long as, and only as long as, she or he is chief of staff. A museum, as a condition of its using park district land, may be required to include the park superintendent as an ex officio director. Depending on the corporate documents and the applicable statutory law, such a director may be a full director, without raising the problems set forth above regarding the honorary director. And the corporate documents may permit such a person to vote.

Often, however, the term "ex officio" is used to describe someone who needs to be recognized (or appeased) and who is not regarded as a fully participating director. All the cautions mentioned with regard to honorary directors (particularly with regard to the attorney-client privilege) apply in such situations; and the ambiguity of the term "ex officio" dictates that its use should be confined to the situation outlined in the preceding paragraph. It is particularly important, in these cases, that the bylaws define the rights and duties of the ex officio director.

B. The Purpose Of Service

1. **All directors must know the corporation's purpose and the persons or interests it serves.**

Any person serving or asked to serve as a director must ask: For what purpose is the corporation maintained? What is the constituency which it is serving? It has been said that all organizations exist to maximize <u>something</u> for <u>somebody</u>: the nonprofit corporation is no exception. Defining the <u>something</u> and the <u>somebody</u> is a duty of every nonprofit board and every director. Once it has been determined <u>what</u> the corporation is maximizing and for <u>whom</u>, all persons serving or asked to serve as directors should determine if these aims are compatible with their reasons for serving on the board.

2. **The corporate documents should record the corporate purpose and the constituency of service and be consistent with actual corporate activities.**

In all nonprofit corporations, the corporate purposes should be stated, at least in general terms, in the articles of incorporation and bylaws. They may also be shaped by a mission statement, adopted by the board, or by undertakings and activities to which corporate assets and energies are committed. Unfortunately, the foregoing places for inquiry may give inconsistent answers, or no answer at all. Although the articles of incorporation will probably control in the event of conflicts of guidance, the director may not find significant teaching there since corporate articles are frequently drawn with as broad a statement of purpose as is legally allowable and the bylaws may be equally vague.

I THE CORPORATION AND ITS DIRECTORS: WHAT THEY DO, HOW THEY DO IT, AND FOR WHOM

If a nonprofit corporation has no instrument which represents a clear statement of its present purposes, a director should urge the creation of such a document. Even where a nonprofit corporation is conducting a specific program or activity, with a clear consensus among its directors, it should be possible to describe that activity and its purpose in a brief mission statement. The articles of incorporation and bylaws may define the broad general purposes of the corporation; but the mission statement should be more specific. As a practical matter, confusion over mission impairs the efficiency of the board in the discharge of its duties.

The detail, the time devoted to the definition of mission, and its documentation will vary with the size and nature of the entity: but all need this element of the corporate structure. We give three examples:

> The board of a small condominium usually operates within a fairly tight structure dictated by its declaration and statutory law; but clear choices may have to be made as to the constituency served (all owners? only owner-occupants?) or the corporate purpose (bare structural maintenance? enhanced value through annual improvements?). A mission statement enables the board to reach these decisions with minimum—or greatly lessened—interpersonal controversy.

> A local community organization—no matter how small—may have to make choices concerning the constituency served: (All residents? Only merchants? Only youth?) or purposes: (All welfare? or specific social services?)

> A major institution, let us say any public benefit corporation with an annual budget of over $500,000, should be able to state the mission to all concerned—donors, the public served, and officials to be satisfied.

The director should not be satisfied with things-as-they-have-been or everyone-knows-why-we're-here.

The board should re-examine its mission and responsibilities from time to time. Any vigorous nonprofit corporation will find that demands and opportunities will continually shape and alter what the corporation actually does; and its surrounding environment will change as well. A periodic examination should be made to determine if the current mission statement is consistent with the articles and bylaws and whether any changes in any of these documents are indicated.

I THE CORPORATION AND ITS DIRECTORS: WHAT THEY DO, HOW THEY DO IT, AND FOR WHOM

C. The Parties To Whom The Director is Accountable

1. All directors are accountable to defined classes of persons or entities

All nonprofit directors are responsible to certain parties; that is to say, some classes of persons or entities have the right to question the director's conduct, even, in extreme cases, bringing him or her into court; and, by implication, there are others who do not have that right.

2. The accountability of directors of mutual benefit corporations is largely equivalent to that of directors of a business corporation

We have emphasized that the nonprofit corporation serves to maximize something for somebody; and the director must be able to identify the something and the somebody. We have also pointed out that the somebody may or may not be the party selecting the director in the first place. In mutual benefit corporations, as a general rule, the somebody involved will be the party or parties who control the tenure of the director—for example, in a trade association the members usually elect the directors—and those same persons will be the parties who may, in appropriate circumstances, call the board of directors to account. Thus, the directors of most mutual benefit corporations hold a relationship to their members much the same as that held by the director of a business corporation to a stockholder.

3. The accountability of directors of public benefit and religious corporations differ from that of mutual benefit corporations

The directors of public benefit and religious corporations are in a different position. From the beginning of public charities (which were originally, in the English speaking world, almost always religious), there was a class of beneficiaries (for example the poor of a parish)—the somebody for whom a charitable corporation was maintained—who were not the parties appointing the director or trustee to office. Furthermore, those beneficiaries were generally deemed incapable of enforcing the director's obligations or were persons who, it was felt, should not have that power. Except for the institutions and procedures outlined herein, this would have left a legal vacuum in which a director would have power without responsibility.

I THE CORPORATION AND ITS DIRECTORS: WHAT THEY DO, HOW THEY DO IT, AND FOR WHOM

4.   The boards of most public benefit corporations are accountable to the state attorney general

Early in the history of charities, under English law, and in the parallel developments in the United States, it was established that the attorney general spoke for the beneficiaries of a charitable trust or corporation and, in effect, became the voice of the somebody for whom a charitable corporation was organized. Under a variety of statutes and constitutional provisions, this role—that of "parens patriae"— continues in the United States, as to both unincorporated charitable trusts and public benefit corporations. In nearly all states, the state attorney general is the party who has authority to call the director of a public benefit or religious corporation to account.

Originally this power related to the enforcement of the public interest in the maintenance of property and funds for the original charitable purpose: preventing a divergence of such funds for improper purposes and intervening if the persons holding such property attempted to change the purpose, even if the new purpose was a proper charitable activity. These powers survive and today a public benefit corporation planning a major change in the use of its assets may be required to consult the attorney general or join him or her in a so-called <u>cy pres</u> proceeding in a court. Statutory provisions have broadened the power of the attorney general in most states to include a general supervision over the solicitation of monies for charitable purposes.

In some states there is a controversy as to whether property held by a corporation, whose purposes are undeniably charitable, is held in trust in the sense that the investment and disbursement of every piece of property is subject to review by the attorney general, or if instead, the attorney general's scrutiny is confined to a review of the overall activities of the corporation to determine whether they are still in furtherance of its basic mission. Generally the attorney general does not assert a right to scrutinize activities of mutual benefit corporations.[4]

5.   Others

The director of a public benefit corporation, such as a conventional charity, will note an omission: we have not listed the donors to the corporation as a party with whom the director has a legal relationship. In general, the omission is correct, although, obviously the corporation will be sensitive to the concerns of its principal donors. There are coming to be exceptions to these generalizations, but it has been, in the past, well established that assets acquired by a charitable corporation without contractual limitations are freed of the donors' control and subject only to the board of directors and to scrutiny by the attorney general as the voice of the parties[5] for whom the corporation conducts its services. Where either the board expects to be responsive to a donor's wishes, or a donor so demands, accountability should be established by specific agreement.

6.   The directors of some public benefit corporations face a mixed accountability

Although the attorney general's powers may extend to all public benefit corporations within a given state, many such corporations have a voting membership to whom the director may be, in part, accountable.

7.   Constitutional considerations limit the public accountability of religious corporations

The directors of religious corporations are generally subject to the foregoing considerations. However, because American constitutional law generally restricts the role of government in dealing with religious corporations to a minimum enforcement of basic fiscal integrity, oversight is more limited, lest the government intrude on freedom of religion.

I THE CORPORATION AND ITS DIRECTORS: WHAT THEY DO, HOW THEY DO IT, AND FOR WHOM

SUGGESTED QUESTIONS REGARDING CHAPTER I

1.   What group of members elected me? If I wasn't elected by a voting membership, how was I elected?

2.   If I was elected by a voting membership, how is that membership defined? Where can I find out: in the bylaws? the Articles of Incorporation? Are the records of voting membership kept in good order? By whom?

3.   When does my term of office expire? Can I be re-elected? Does my term run until a specific date, or until my successor is chosen?

4.   Can I be removed from my position as director? By whom? On what basis?

5.   Was I selected by some group of members or some entity which differs from the source of tenure of the other directors?

6.   What is our corporation supposed to do and for whom?

7.   Does the corporation have a mission statement?

8.   When was that statement last reviewed?

9.   What parties or officials can question what we do as directors of the corporation?

THE NONPROFIT CORPORATION'S CHECKLIST: CHAPTER I

Note: For purposes of simplicity in these checklists, we describe a corporation with a Chair, who presides over the Board of Directors; a Chief Executive, who may be a staff person; an Executive Committee; a Nominating Committee, and an Audit Committee. We also assume a Legal Counsel—someone, paid or unpaid, having primary responsibility for the Corporation's legal affairs. Many corporations have other Committees established for specific purposes, such as reviewing staff performance, fixing compensation, monitoring compliance with legal requirements and periodic review of bylaws. In many corporations the Executive Committee performs most or all of the functions, and these checklists will so assume.

SUBJECT	TO BE REVIEWED BY WHOM	HOW OFTEN	COMMENT
Basic Documents			
1. Review of the Articles of Incorporation.	a) Full Board, with Legal Counsel b) by the new director	a) Periodic review, probably every three years b) On joining board	Review should include: conformity to corporate mission; compliance with tax and corporate laws; any explicit provisions relating to directors and officers.
2. Review of the Bylaws:	In general: a) In large corporations: Legal Counsel or Executive Committee, responding to Board b) by the new director	In general: a) Periodic review, probably every three years b) On joining board	Review should include: Conformity to corporate mission; Problems possibly arising from changes in program; compliance with tax and corporate laws; any explicit provisions relating to directors and officers, including indemnification, insurance and availability of limitations on liability

THE NONPROFIT CORPORATION'S CHECKLIST: CHAPTER I

SUBJECT	TO BE REVIEWED BY WHOM	HOW OFTEN	COMMENT
a. Is the number of directors stated in the Bylaws in conformity with the number actually serving (or the size the board will reach if new directors are elected)?	Chief Executive; and Nominating Committee,	Annually in all cases; always before notice goes out for meeting to elect directors	This is a frequent problem, particularly in smaller public benefit corporations.
b. Are there officers serving who bear titles or perform functions that are not reflected in the bylaws? For example, is the Chief Executive's function described therein?	Chief Executive and Nominating Committee	Annually in all cases; always before notice goes out of meeting to elect directors	Many public benefit corporations have bylaws describing as "President" an uncompensated person who simply presides over the board. In many nonprofits, Chief Executive's functions are not described in bylaws; they should be.
c. Do the bylaws have a statement of corporate mission or purpose consistent with the Articles of Incorporation, or other mission statement?	Chief Executive	Annually and every time either of these documents is changed	Bylaws may have no statement of purpose and there does not have to be one; but if there is one, it should be consistent with other documents.

THE NONPROFIT CORPORATION'S CHECKLIST: CHAPTER I

	SUBJECT	TO BE REVIEWED BY WHOM	HOW OFTEN	COMMENT
d.	Are there, or should there be, Honorary Directors?	Chair and Chief Executive	Probably every three or four years.	Voting rights (or lack thereof) should be clearly defined and understood.
e.	If the corporation has members (as defined in this Guidebook, that is members with voting rights) is there an accurate list of the members consistent with whatever definition of eligibility is contained in the bylaws?	Chief Executive	At least annually, and before notice goes out for any meeting where elections are to be held	There is probably no area with greater compliance problems than this. Nonprofits, particularly Public Benefit and Religious Corporations, will often designate as "members" persons who are simply donors or friends, keeping no accurate records thereof. The rights (or lack thereof) of such persons to vote should be clearly defined and any problems reviewed with Legal Counsel.
3.	Review of a corporate mission statement;	Chief Executive reporting to Board.	Probably every three or four years	If there is no mission statement, create one.
a.	Is there a single statement; in what document is it embodied?	Chief Executive reporting to Board	Probably every three or four years	There should be a single overall statement; separate statements for individual programs may be in order, but they should be consistent.

THE NONPROFIT CORPORATION'S CHECKLIST: CHAPTER I

SUBJECT	TO BE REVIEWED BY WHOM	HOW OFTEN	COMMENT
b. Are the corporation's public statements (e.g., brochures, press releases, etc.) as issued during the last year, consistent with the mission statement?	Chief Executive	Annually, and as each brochure or press release is issued	Nonprofits dealing with public controversies will often find problems here.
c. Has the Board reviewed the mission statement and understood the constituency served by the corporation?	Chair, bringing issue to Board	Probably every three or four years	Board should always understand that it has a specific constituency or service.

ENDNOTES

1. (p. 7) The obvious analogy is that of a representative in Congress, who may, on the floor or through committee, exert immense influence on the actions of government, but is given no function, under our Constitution, when acting alone. But (again paralleling a member of Congress) the individual director has legally protected rights to participate in corporate decisions and has legally recognized rights and duties to be informed concerning corporate transactions.

2. (p. 7) A one-person board of directors is permitted under some state statutes; where such a board exists, the single director's act is an exercise of the board's powers. The Model Act (§ 8.03) (and most state statutes) requires a minimum of three directors.

3. (p. 7) These categories are not mutually exclusive: a person who is a director of a nonprofit corporation may also be a member, having, as an individual, whatever rights a member may have in the corporation, just as she or he may also be an officer or agent; but as a director, the individual acts on behalf of others.

4. (p. 13) The reader should remember that the classifications of corporations as "public benefit," "religious" or "mutual benefit" are not watertight. See Introduction, p. 3; Olson and Hatch, Director and Officer Liability (1991) ¶ 11.01 et seq.; Kurtz, Board Liability (1988) 91-100.

5. (p. 13) See Newman v. Forward Lands, 430 F. Supp. 1320 (E.D. Pa. 1977) (". . . someone with a special interest may sue . . ."), citing Restatement of the Law, Second, Trusts (1959), § 391. The Restatement makes clear that the donor cannot sue to enforce a charitable trust and is not someone with a "special interest." The Restatement deals with charitable trusts, not with corporations: but the principles of accountability would be, in this instance, much the same.

II

DUTIES OF DIRECTORS

A. The Standards Of Conduct Applicable To The Individual Corporate Director

In carrying out their functions for the corporation are subject to two primary obligations: a Duty of Care and a Duty of Loyalty.

The Duties of Care and Loyalty are the common terms for the standards which guide all actions a director takes. These standards are derived from a century of litigation principally involving business corporations and are equally applicable to nonprofit corporations.

B. The Duty Of Care

The Duty of Care calls upon a director to participate in the decisions of the board and to be informed as to data relevant to such decisions.

A common statement of the Duty of Care asks a director (1) to be reasonably informed; (2) to participate in decisions; and (3) to do so in good faith and with the care of an ordinarily prudent person in similar circumstances.[1]

Each of the tasks outlined below requires the _efficient_ allocation of time by the director: the suggestions we give as to each element of the director's function must all be evaluated in light of this need. Although we cannot say that any one of these tasks is essential (i.e., that a failure to complete the particular function automatically demonstrates a failure of care) substantial compliance with these elements of care is commonly expected of the nonprofit director and may be required by law.

1. **The Duty of Care requires that a director be informed and exercise independent judgment.**

To discharge the Duty of Care the director must monitor the organization's activities. Such participation finds expression in such things as:

II DUTIES OF DIRECTORS

a. Attending Meetings

Regular attendance at meetings of the board of directors is a basic element of prudent performance as a director.

All directors must remember that they act as a group, and therefore attendance at board and committee meetings is urged. Continuous or repeated absence may expose the director to the risk of not satisfying the Duty of Care. Sporadic board attendance by some directors reduces the morale of those who do attend. It should be recognized, however, that directors also render a great deal of service outside board meetings by taking on various assignments for the organization or the board, by opening doors, by soliciting contributions, etc.[2]

It should be understood that, in most states, directors cannot vote or participate by appointing another person, even another director, as a proxy.[3] All directors should understand the reasons for this rule. First of all, whatever reasons a director's constituency may have had for choosing her or him, that choice was the selection of one person to perform a duty, not the grant of a transferable privilege. Secondly, all the other directors are entitled to demand the duly elected or appointed director's wisdom and judgment, not that of such surrogate as the director may choose. Thirdly, such deference and accommodation the directors themselves may give to each other in the course of their work cannot, as a practical matter, be transferred to purely personal appointees.[4]

If a board of directors encounters significant problems concerning the frequency of a director's attendance, it should consider adopting or recommending bylaws or policies permitting or requiring the removal of directors who regularly miss meetings or attend only portions of meetings, or create honorary directorships or advisory councils for such persons.

b. Independent Judgment

Each director, no matter how selected, shares in all the responsibilities and powers of the directors. Each director should exercise her or his independent judgment on all corporate decisions.

The law conceives of a board of directors as an entity, each member of which shares the same rights and the same duties, and each member of which is accountable to the same constituency. Even if other parties may regard the director as representing a particular group or interest, these considerations do not affect his or her duties as a director which are to the entire organization and the responsibilities will be the same as those of any other director. If the board decides to delegate a task to a particular director, that is a decision of the board, not of the constituency or body which selected or suggested the director.

II DUTIES OF DIRECTORS

c.   Information

To function effectively a director needs to be informed.

To function effectively, a director needs to have an adequate source of information flow. This information is generally supplied by the staff. To the extent that it is not adequate, a board or an individual director will have to determine what additional information is needed. Needless to say, the director should read the information with which he or she is supplied.

In some small nonprofit entities, such as neighborhood improvement bodies or condominium associations, the board itself may be its own primary source of information. With larger organizations, however, the board will inevitably use and rely on information prepared by the corporation's officers and agents. This means that the corporation's staff will unavoidably have a significant effect on the board's decisions since, inevitably, the staff must select much of the information the directors receive. Even when a director has total and justified confidence in the suppliers of information, he or she should be at least aware of this.

In general, the Board may rely on information supplied by the staff, but if for any reason any member of the Board thinks that it is inadequate in any respect, he or she should not hesitate to request further information. Such requests should be reasonable and should not overwhelm the staff.

2.   Reliance

In the ordinary course of business, a director may act in reliance on information and reports received from regular sources whom the director reasonably regards as trustworthy.

A director may rely upon the reports, communications and information received from another director, a committee or from any officer, employee or agent if the director reasonably believes the source to be reliable and competent.[5] The Model Act expressly recognizes the concept of reliance on others and thus attempts to codify a somewhat diffuse common law standard:

> "In discharging his or her duties, a director is entitled to rely on information, opinions, reports or statements, including financial statements and other financial data, if prepared or presented by:

II DUTIES OF DIRECTORS

(1)   one or more officers or employees of the corporation whom the director reasonably believes to be reliable and competent in the matters presented;

(2)   legal counsel, public accountants or other persons as to matters the director reasonably believes are within the person's professional or expert competence;

(3)   a committee of the board of which the director is not a member, as to matters within its jurisdiction, if the director reasonably believes the committee merits confidence; or

(4)   in the case of religious corporations, religious authorities and ministers, priests, rabbis or other persons whose position or duties in the religious organization the director believes justify reliance and confidence and whom the director believes to be reliable and competent in the matters presented."

(Model Act, Section 8.30(b))

However, the director will not be acting in good faith if she or he has such knowledge about the matter in question as would make such reliance unreasonable. (Model Act, Section 8.30(c))

3.   **Delegation**

The board of directors, as such, does not operate the day to day business of the corporation. In delegating that function to others, it must set policies and oversee the corporate agents.

The principles of delegation stated above apply to the board as a whole; the individual director may not delegate his or her responsibilities as a director. A director cannot vote by proxy.

The board of directors is not expected to operate the corporation on a day-to-day basis. Even under statutes providing that the business and affairs of a corporation shall be "managed" by the board of directors, it is recognized that actual operation is a function of "management," that is, the officers and agents of the corporation. In conventional corporate theory, the responsibility of the board is limited to overseeing such operations. This principle does not relieve the board of its monitoring responsibilities, but directors are not personally responsible for actions or omissions of officers, employees or agents of the

II DUTIES OF DIRECTORS

corporation as long as such persons have been prudently selected and the directors have relied reasonably upon such officers, employees or agents.

While in the business corporation world, the board often makes clear written delegations of authority to the chief executive and other officers, this is not the norm in the nonprofit world. It is suggested that nonprofits corporations give consideration to making more formal delegations of authority to the chief executive officer (who would then be free to sub-delegate portions of it). Among other things, such a process might serve to keep some directors from improperly interfering with management prerogatives, a distressing but not uncommon occurrence in the nonprofit world.

In small nonprofit corporations, this general model of delegation may be difficult to achieve, particularly where "management" may not be continuing full time persons but rather a series of separate contractors or agents. Where a member of the board occupies both the role of a director and that of an agent, our theoretical model treats that person, while acting in his or her capacity as an agent, just as the law would treat such a person who is not serving on the board.[6]

C. Discharging The Duty Of Care: Some Practical Suggestions

A board should examine how it can most efficiently use the limited time its members can devote to its functions.

In all but the smallest and simplest corporations, the corporation's needs for the board's attention will often exceed the time the board has to furnish this resource. Hence this limited asset must be used efficiently.

1.   The Schedule Of Meetings

Meetings of the board of directors should meet on a regular basis.

The importance of attendance at meetings has been noted. The board should meet on a regular basis. The schedule of board meetings should be fixed at the beginning of each year so that each board member can place the meetings on his or her calendar well in advance and thus assure attendance.

The practical frequency for a board meeting will also depend on the size of the corporation, the geographic nature of its constituency, budgetary considerations and other constraints. But none of these considerations detract from the need for regularity or preclude the possibility thereof.

II DUTIES OF DIRECTORS

Meetings held "only as the need arises" or "upon demand" are rarely satisfactory. Directors should be reluctant to serve on a board which meets only at the pleasure of some officer or committee or where meetings are held only annually.

The Model Act (§ 8.21) permits the directors to act without a meeting, by unanimous written consent. Most state statutes have similar provisions; and such a procedure may frequently be appropriate in the transaction of routine business. Directors should, however, be cautious about the ratification or authorization of major activities or decisions without a meeting. While this is sometimes necessary, it should not be a substitute for regular meetings.

2. The Schedule of Information

As much information as practical should be provided on a regular schedule.

Information should be provided to the Board in a timely manner, so that the Board will have a realistic opportunity to review and consider it. These needs will be more easily and efficiently satisfied if the directors establish a regularly scheduled system of reports and data for those corporate activities which are sufficiently repetitive to be predictable to all parties. These will include financial reports, program reports, and the like. Just as with board meetings, information which is unnecessarily sporadic and unprogrammed is inefficient and substantially inferior in value. Furthermore, in almost all such situations, some board member is receiving information, and thus inequalities within the board are created. All directors should recognize that any control over the distribution of information is unavoidably a partial control over decisions to be made; any control over the timing of information is likewise a political act. Since some controls over distribution and timing are inevitable, regularity is an essential check and balance.

Distribution of as much material as possible in advance of the board meeting (preferably by the week-end before the meeting) should be the objective. Certain types of reports, particularly financial reports, should be furnished on a regular schedule, whether monthly, quarterly or semi-annually.

All of the above considerations should be balanced by a judgment as to the staff time required to prepare the information. The preparation of meaningful data for a board meeting consumes significant amounts of time. The board should be mindful of this in defining the information it requires.

II DUTIES OF DIRECTORS

3. The Rules of Procedure

The board should adopt rules of procedure appropriate to its size, the constituencies represented on the board and the diversity of its membership.

Any working board will work out its own standard agenda for board meetings and the degree of formality, or lack thereof, used in submitting motions, amendments to resolutions, recording votes, etc. However, matters of substantial importance should always be acted on by formal resolution and the vote recorded in the minutes, even in the smallest and most closely-knit board.

4. The Business Judgment Rule

Even where a corporate action has proven to be unwise or unsuccessful, a director will be protected from liability arising therefrom if he or she acted in good faith and in a manner reasonably believed to be in the corporation's best interest, and with independent and informed judgment.

A director exercising good faith judgment will usually be protected from liability to the corporation or to its membership under the Business Judgment Rule.[7] This legal concept is well established in the case law applying to business corporations. It has also been recognized as applicable to the directors of nonprofit corporations and it seems probable that it will become generally so applied.[8] The Rule states that a court, in an action brought by the corporation or its internal constituency, will not re-examine the actions of a director in authorizing or permitting a corporate action if such director's action was undertaken in good faith in a manner reasonably believed to be in the best interests of the corporation, and with an independent and informed judgment. The doctrine basically is a statement by the courts that it is inappropriate for them to "second guess" corporate management.

The Business Judgment Rule will not be applied in situations where basic breaches of duty by the director (such as criminal activity, fraud, bad faith, wilful and wanton misconduct) are present.[9]

5. Legal Requirements.

In discharging the duty of care, the board should not be unmindful of the legal requirements to which the corporation may be subject, particularly in a regulated environment such as the health care industry.

II DUTIES OF DIRECTORS

D. The Duty Of Loyalty

The Duty of Loyalty requires directors to exercise their powers in the interest of the corporation not in their own interest or the interest of another entity or person.

By assuming office, the director acknowledges that with regard to any corporate activity the best interests of the corporation must prevail over the director's individual interests or the particular interests of the constituency selecting him or her. The basic legal principle to be observed here is a negative one: the director shall not use a corporate position for individual personal advantage. The Duty of Loyalty primarily relates to:

- Conflicts of Interest,

- Corporate Opportunity, and

- Confidentiality.

1. Conflict Of Interest: General Principles

Directors of nonprofit corporations may have interests in conflict with those of the corporation. The Duty of Loyalty requires that a director be conscious of the potential for such conflicts and act with candor and care in dealing with such situations.

Conflicts of interest involving a director are not inherently illegal nor are they to be regarded as a reflection on the integrity of the board or of the director. It is the manner in which the director and the board deals with a disclosed conflict which determines the propriety of the transaction.

A man or woman active in professional or community life, while serving on a nonprofit board, will on occasion encounter situations where her or his duty to the nonprofit corporation may affect or be affected by personal interests or obligations to some other person or entity.

A conflict of interest is present whenever a director has a material personal interest in a proposed contract or transaction to which the corporation may be a party. This interest can occur either directly or indirectly. The director may be personally involved with the transaction, or may have an employment or investment relationship with an entity with which the corporation is dealing, or it may arise from some family relationship. A conflict of interest may result from a director performing professional services for the organization. For example, a banker, insurance agent, attorney or real estate broker may benefit from employment by the organization. The board should not assume that a conflict cannot exist for a director who receives no monetary or other tangible benefit from a transaction with the corporation. For example, access to information which could be used for individual profit might put the director in conflict with the corporation.

The purpose of the procedures outlined in this chapter, of written policies, and of conflict disclosure statements is not to prevent dishonest individuals from behaving dishonestly; no legal procedures will achieve that. Rather, we seek to encourage and help honest and loyal people to act accordingly and to perform their duties in a manner required by law or suggested by good corporate practice.

The law recognizes these problems, not by treating conflict as inherently a moral or legal offence, but rather by prescribing the methods whereby a board of directors and the individual directors should disclose conflicts and how they should proceed in the face of such situations. In general a director's conflict will be cleared of any consequence by, first, full disclosure and, second, approval or ratification of the subject action by a disinterested majority of directors. The issue is treated in detail in Model Act § 8.31 and the Comment thereon. Although particular state statutes may differ from the Model Act, the issues addressed therein are an excellent guide.

2. Conflict Of Interest: Awareness And Disclosure

A director should be sensitive to any interest he or she may have in a decision to be made by the board of directors and, as far as possible, recognize such interest prior to the discussion or presentation of such a matter before the board.

When a director has an interest in a transaction being considered by the board of directors, the director should disclose the conflict before the board of directors takes action on the matter.

Upon disclosure by the director, the board should provide a disinterested review of the matter.

The foregoing principles should guide the board and its members: the first rule is awareness, the second disclosure, and the third is disinterested review. To implement these principles the board should consider the adoption of a written policy on conflicts.

For corporations of any size it is desirable to have a statement of policy or appropriate questionnaire signed by each of the directors, as well as by each of the officers and employees who are in a position of control or are involved in policy making decisions.

II DUTIES OF DIRECTORS

Appendix A contains a sample of such a policy statement and questionnaire. It should be noted, however, that the forms set forth in Appendix A call for an annual disclosure. The board should also establish a procedure for conflicts arising in individual and episodic situations.

Each material conflict of interest disclosure should be in writing and fully recorded in the minutes. In addition, related party transactions may have to be disclosed to the Internal Revenue Service.

The duty of <u>disclosure</u> of an interest exists without regard to whether the proposed transaction is fair, or whether the director urges or opposes the transaction, or whether the director is present during discussion of the transaction, votes thereon or abstains from voting, or is counted or not counted in establishing a quorum at any meeting where the transaction is discussed.

It is true that many statutes uphold the validity of a transaction authorized even when a director had an <u>undisclosed</u> interest therein, if the transaction was "fair" (e.g., Model Act Section 8.31(a)); but in the event of litigation, the non-disclosing director, and, in some instances, even the disinterested directors who supported the transaction, will have the burden of proving fairness. As a practical matter, a non-disclosing director exposes him or herself and the board to substantial risks in such an undisclosed conflict. While the law affords protection to directors whose decisions were made in the ordinary course of business and in good faith, however unfortunate the decisions may turn out to be, this doctrine (the Business Judgment Rule, described above) will not extend to shield the non-disclosing director or the director who does not reasonably inform him or herself.

Disclosure enables the other members of the board to evaluate the proposed transaction not merely in terms of fairness, but also for its impact on the public image of the corporation.

Generally, the disclosure should include the existence of such interest and its nature (e.g. those arising from financial or family relationships, or professional or business affiliations, etc.) and should be made before any action is taken by the board concerning the matter. The director may consider it prudent to be absent from that part of the meeting when the matter is being discussed except when her or his information may be needed. A director having a conflict should record his or her absence from discussion and abstention from a vote relating thereto.

In some cases a director may have an interest in a transaction but be unable, because of duties running to others, to disclose the nature of the interest. In such a case, the director should at least state that such an interest exists, consider leaving the meeting, or at least abstain from the discussion and not vote thereon. Where the conflicting interest presents so difficult a problem that even the above measures are impossible, the director should consider resigning.

In addition, an interested director should be aware that appropriate voting and quorum requirements must be met. In many states, a director, even if interested, may be counted for the purpose of determining the presence of a quorum, but such director's vote is not permitted to be counted as an authorization of the matter; in some states the interested director is not permitted to vote thereon.

A board of directors which discovers that it has acted upon a proposal in ignorance of an undisclosed interest therein should promptly reexamine the issue, with an appropriate record of such scrutiny.

3.   Conflict Of Interest: The Nature of Personal Interest

We have referred to the impropriety of a director's using her or his position to advance a "personal" interest. At the same time we recognize that the very reasons why a particular director is selected may relate to that director's concern for, and knowledge of, the particular business of the corporation. A personal interest rising to the point of a conflict to be disclosed might arise in situations such as the following:

> A director of an art museum may have—and probably should have—definite opinions as to the priority, in new purchases, of contemporary American painting versus Old Masters. The director's opinion and preferences present no conflict.

> If the director was generally a collector of contemporary painting and the museum was faced with a particular possible acquisition in that field of art, the director's personal interests might rise to the point requiring disclosure.

> A director of a trade association might have been selected because of his or her familiarity with the impact of Pacific Rim competition on the products of the association's members. Her or his urging that the association advocate a particular tariff bill would present no problem even if the director's own company would benefit along with others.

> If the director's own company was one of the relatively small group of manufacturers affected by Pacific imports, but most of the associations's members were untouched thereby, a decision to divert association assets and influence on behalf of that minority might present a material conflict.

II DUTIES OF DIRECTORS

4.   The Treatment of Insider Transactions

In some cases a board may legitimately choose to deal with an inside supplier of goods and services because of greater familiarity with the supplier's reliability. Although such association with a director providing services may result in extra benefits for the corporation, the corporate records must show that the best interests of the corporation were the overriding consideration in deciding to use such a supplier.

5.   Corporate Opportunity

Before a director engages in a transaction which he or she reasonably should know may be of interest to the corporation, the director should disclose the transaction to the board of directors in sufficient detail and adequate time to enable the board to act or decline to act with regard to such transaction.

A corporate opportunity arises when a director knows that he or she can participate in a transaction which would plausibly fall within the corporation's present or future activities. As a matter of good corporate practice, the director should affirmatively present the opportunity to the board before participating in the transaction outside the corporation.[10] Although legal requirements as to these transactions vary from state to state, a director should, for her or his self-protection, and as a matter of good corporate practice, make a clear record of such disclosure and request that the board's abstention (if any) from exercise of the opportunity be explicit and of record.

E. Confidentiality

A director should not, in the regular course of business, disclose information about the corporation's legitimate activities unless they are already known by the public or are of public record.

In the normal course of business, a director should treat as confidential all matters involving the corporation until there has been general public disclosure or unless the information is a matter of public record or common knowledge. The individual director is not a spokesperson for the corporation and thus disclosure to the public of corporate activities should be made only through the corporation's designated spokesperson, usually the Chief Executive or, in large organizations, a public relations officer. This presumption of confidential treatment should apply to all current information about legitimate board or corporate activities.[11]

II DUTIES OF DIRECTORS

SUGGESTED QUESTIONS AS TO DUTIES OF DIRECTORS

1.   How often does our board meet? Is this according to a regular schedule?

2.   How frequently have I attended, or can I attend in the future, regular board meetings?

3.   What information is given to me in advance of each board meeting? Is it relevant to decisions to be reached at the meeting?

4.   Am I satisfied with the information I have received? As to quantity? As to subject? As to reliability? Is it too little? Is it more than I can really analyze between my receipt of it and the board meeting?

5.   Is there any information submitted to me which I feel is incomplete or untrustworthy? How do I deal with this problem?

6.   Who manages, in the day to day sense, the business of the corporation?

7.   Do I have an interest—personal or business—that conflicts with the interests of the corporation?

8.   Has an occasion arisen where I should disclose that interest?

9.   Do I know of a conflict involving another director? Did she or he disclose that problem?

10.   Does our corporation have a policy on conflict disclosure? Is it in writing? Do we sign a disclosure statement relating to this subject?

THE NONPROFIT CORPORATION'S CHECKLIST: CHAPTER II

Note: For purposes of simplicity in these checklists, we describe a corporation with a Chair, who presides over the Board of Directors; a Chief Executive, who may be a staff person; an Executive Committee; a Nominating Committee; and an Audit Committee. We also assume a Legal Counsel—someone, paid or unpaid, having primary responsibility for the Corporation's legal affairs. Many corporations have other Committees established for specific purposes, such as reviewing staff performance, fixing compensation, monitoring compliance with legal requirements and periodic review of bylaws. In many corporations the Executive Committee performs most or all of the functions, and these checklists will so assume.

	SUBJECT	TO BE REVIEWED BY WHOM	HOW OFTEN	COMMENT
A.	**The Board's Record Of Services**			
1.	What is the record of each director's attendance at board meetings?	Chair, Chief Executive, Nominating Committee	Before submission of nominations for election; from time to time during year	Regular attendance serves to maintain an active board of high morale.
2.	What members of the board have missed half the meetings during the last 12 months?	Chair, Chief Executive and Nominating Committee	Before submission of nominations for election; from time to time during year	If the number is large, see below.
3.	Does the board have, or should it examine having, a provision for removal of a director who fails (without adequate excuse) to reach a minimum record of attendance?	Chair, Chief Executive and Nominating Committee	Whenever there is review of bylaws	Sometimes the simple proposal of such a bylaw will trigger appropriate resignations. Even if actual removals are accomplished by requested resignations, a bylaw provision may be desirable.

THE NONPROFIT CORPORATION'S CHECKLIST: CHAPTER II

	SUBJECT	TO BE REVIEWED BY WHOM	HOW OFTEN	COMMENT
4.	How many board meetings took place in the last 12 months? Were all the meetings called for in the bylaws actually held?	Chair and Chief Executive	At least annually	The optimum number of board meetings is to be determined by needs, but a quarterly meeting schedule is recommended as a minimum.
5.	Is there any feeling on the part of the members of the board that this number of meetings is inadequate for complete review of the corporation's business?	Chair and Board	Annually	This question is closely related to the Committee structure of the corporation.
6.	Should the number of meetings be reduced?	Chair and Board	Annually	
7.	Would more adequate review be obtained by delegating more duties to committees?	Chair and Board	Annually	See Chapter IV
8.	How many directors have contributed funds to the corporation? Have all done so? What is the average?	Chief Executive and Nominating Committee of any corporation soliciting funds.	Annually, and before any re-election or renomination of directors.	

THE NONPROFIT CORPORATION'S CHECKLIST: CHAPTER II

SUBJECT	TO BE REVIEWED BY WHOM	HOW OFTEN	COMMENT
9. What has been the attendance record of the members of the corporation's committees?	Chief Executive and Nominating Committee	Annually; if committees are elected or appointed on a schedule, before such election or appointment.	Attendance record at Committees should be part of Director's record reviewed for any re-election decision.
B. The Corporation's Policies on Conflicts			
1. Do we have a conflict policy statement which all directors and officers are expected to execute?	Full Board	Annually	The implication is obvious; if there isn't one, there should be.
a. Should it be reviewed for substantive content?	Legal Counsel and Audit Committee; then full Board	Annually	Review by full board should test its understanding of statement.
b. Was it, in fact, signed by all directors?	Audit Committee	Annually and at point at which each new director joins board	Statement should be re-executed every year.
c. How does the corporation deal with conflicts that arise between the execution dates of a regular conflict statement?	Chief Executive reporting to Board	As often as conflicts arise; review of totality annually	Full and prompt reporting is essential.

THE NONPROFIT CORPORATION'S CHECKLIST: CHAPTER II

SUBJECT	TO BE REVIEWED BY WHOM	HOW OFTEN	COMMENT
2. Was there a meeting at which a director disclosed a conflict of interest regarding a decision?	Legal Counsel and Audit Committee	The disclosure should precede or be simultaneous with the decision	Corporate minutes must record this event.
a. If we did, was there an adequate record in the minutes of that disclosure?	Legal Counsel and Audit Committee	As often as such disclosure occurs	Corporate minutes must record this event.
b. Was there a vote on the issue to which the director had a conflict?	Legal Counsel and Audit Committee	As often as such disclosure occurs	Corporate minutes must record this event.
c. If so, was there a quorum (as defined by the statute of incorporation) for such vote?	Legal Counsel and Audit Committee	At meeting in question	State statutes vary as to how quorum and proper votes are determined in these situations.
d. If so, was there a vote of an adequate number of disinterested directors?	Chair, Legal Counsel	At meeting in question	Resolution should pass without needing vote of conflicted director.

ENDNOTES

1.	(p. 21) The Model Act § 8.30(a) states: "A director shall discharge his or her duties as a director, including his or her duties as a member of a committee: (1) in good faith; (2) with the care an ordinarily prudent person in a like position would exercise under similar circumstances; and (3) in a manner the director reasonably believes to be in the best interests of the corporation."

	The Model Act Comment to § 8.30 states "The concept of 'under similar circumstances' relates not only to the circumstances of the corporation but to the special background, qualifications, and management experience of the individual director and the role the director plays in the corporation. In many public benefit corporations an important role of directors is fund-raising. Many directors are elected to the board to raise money or because of financial contributions they have made to the corporation. These individuals may have no particular skill or background that otherwise would be helpful to the corporation. No special skill or expertise should be expected from such directors unless their background or knowledge evidences some special ability. Such individuals upon becoming directors are obligated to act as directors and may not simply act as figureheads ignoring problems. However, their role should be considered in determining whether they have met their obligations under section 8.30."

	Some states would assume a minimum level of competence for all directors, regardless of skill, experience or ability.

2.	(p. 22) The Model Act (§ 8.20(c)) and many state statutes permit a director to attend a meeting by telephonic communication. Clearly, a director so participating is meeting the requirements of attendance.

3.	(p. 22) A small number of jurisdictions are exceptions to this statement. If a board wishes to permit a "representative" of a director to attend a meeting or even participate in the discussion therein, that courtesy (it is that, and nothing more) cannot confer any right to vote at the meeting. The board should understand that the presence of such a representative raises the same problems previously discussed as to honorary directors. See Chapter I, A, supra.

4.	(p. 22) A few state statutes provide for the election of alternate directors who can serve in the absence of the principal director. See Pa. C.S.A. (Purdon, 1991) § 5725(d). Where such an office exists, the alternate properly present at a meeting is not a proxy, and none of the problems noted in the text would arise.

5.	(p. 23) It should be noted that the Comment to the Model Act § 8.30 states: "In order to rely on a report a director must have read it, been present at a meeting where it was presented or otherwise have evaluated it."

6.	(p. 25) Some commentators analyzing the activities of Public Benefit Corporations, assert that effective nonprofit management requires a more overlapping role for the board and management. See Houle, Governing Boards, (1989), pp. 86 et seq.

7.	(p. 27) The Rule, as applied to business corporations, is treated in detail in Block, Barton & Radin, The Business Judgment Rule (3rd ed. 1989) and Olsen & Hatch, Director and Officer Liability (1991). Although these authorities give little attention to nonprofit corporations, the standards described are generally applicable to nonprofit directors. See discussion in Kurtz, Board Liability (1988) 49-59.

8.	(p. 27) Although cases explicitly mentioning the Rule in a nonprofit context are few, the standards used by the courts in nonprofit cases are clearly derived from the business context. See, for example, Beard v. Achenbach Memorial Hospital, 170 F.2d 859 (C.A. 10, 1948)

9.	(p. 27) See Stern v. Lucy Webb Hayes National Training School for Deaconesses & Missionaries, 381 F. Supp. 1003, 1013 (D.D.C. 1974); Beard v. Achenbach Memorial Hospital Association, 170 F.2d 859, 862 (C.A. 10, 1948).

10.	(p. 32) Valle v. North Jersey Automobile Club, 141 N.J. Super. 573, 359 A.2d 504 (App. Div. 1976).

11.	(p. 32) Some public benefit corporations already face, and probably will increasingly face, demands for open meetings of their boards; in some cases, mixed public-private activities may impose that duty. Such practices are, as of this writing, infrequently required as a matter of law: but if open meetings are adopted as a practice, specific rules as to confidentiality, whether or not legally mandated, will have to be developed. See Baughman, Trustees, Trusteeship and the Public Good, Quorum Books, 1987, pp. 52, 155.

	A somewhat different issue is raised by the many statutes governing condominiums which require that all board meetings (with narrowly defined exceptions) be open to owners. e.g., Ill. Rev. Stat., ch. 30 § 18 (9). In such cases, of course, the board meets in the presence of those to whom it is accountable.

III

DIRECTORS' RIGHTS
AND SPECIAL PROBLEMS

A. Directors' Rights

As a corollary to all the previously described responsibilities, the director has rights appropriate to the discharge of those obligations.

1.   **Management Access.** Within the bounds of reason, board members should feel free to contact the Chief Executive or the secretary of the board if such a position exists on the staff. Board members should be more restrained in contacting other members of management and should be cognizant of management's role, of not interfering with it, and of not undercutting the Chief Executive or other officers. Directors, while serving as volunteers, should be especially careful not to make demands or requests of staff which would be inappropriate for other volunteers.

2.   **Books and Records.** A director has a right to inspect, for reasonable purposes and at reasonable intervals, the corporation's books and records and to be provided with requested data derived therefrom. A board member may reasonably require that her or his accountant or attorney have access to such data.

3.   **Notice.** All directors should be given ample advance notice of all meetings.

4.   **Minutes.** All directors should be given a copy of minutes of all meetings of the full board and any executive committee if that committee is exercising board powers. Except for the minutes of the executive committee, which generally acts in place of the whole board, and except for the minutes of committees of which he or she is a member, a director usually will be satisfied with a review of only the summarized reports of committees which are submitted to the whole board. However, a review of other minutes is a useful way of keeping informed, and a director has a right to receive them on request.

5.   **Committee Meetings**

The board should consider a policy concerning attendance at committee meetings by directors not serving on the committee. Whether to permit or forbid attendance by non-members, or to forbid for one committee and permit, or even encourage attendance at another, is a decision which will vary with each corporation.

III DIRECTORS' RIGHTS AND SPECIAL PROBLEMS

B. The Director With Knowledge Of Illegal Activities

A director may not ignore what he or she believes to be illegal activity.

When a director believes that a corporate activity may be illegal, he or she should proceed as follows:

> First, if the subject activity is ongoing, or is about to take place, the issue should be drawn to the attention of the chief executive with a demand for action or investigation; and if he or she fails to respond, the issue should go to the full board;

> Second, if, after a board discussion, the activity is not repudiated, or if the activity is a past event of which the director was previously unaware, the director's dissent should be clearly recorded in the minutes; and the director may wish to consult his or her counsel to determine if·further disclosure outside the corporation is required, or if she or he should resign.

C. The Director As Trustee

Nonprofit corporation law in most states treats conflicts of interest as a recurrent problem to be dealt with by certain guidelines and disclosures. However, the law of trusts, as a general rule, regards a trustee's self-dealing as inherently voidable, regardless of motives or objective fairness. Furthermore, the trustee's power to delegate may be narrowly limited; a director, as has been shown, may delegate some functions. Although a director is generally not a trustee, he or she may, while not actually being such, be held to the same standard in such situations as:

- The corporation may hold an endowment fund designated for specific purposes, which may require the directors to invest and manage it separately;

- Similarly, the directors may be responsible for carrying out the terms of a gift or bequest;

- In certain circumstances, under both state and federal law, an employer corporation has obligations analogous to those of a trustee with regard to employee benefit plans; and

III DIRECTORS' RIGHTS AND SPECIAL PROBLEMS

- A public benefit or religious corporation seeking to change its purpose or function may be faced with assertions that it holds its assets in trust for its original mission, and some states do so hold. A so-called "cy pres" proceeding may be necessary in order to reallocate resources.

The director will inevitably be confused with the nomenclature here. In the first place, some nonprofit corporations, particularly in the public benefit field, may call their directors "trustees" without intending to confer any special powers or impose any special duties in so doing. Secondly, an assertion that an organization holds some program or asset "in trust" for someone or something is a common, if exaggerated, metaphor arising in public controversies. Assets held by a corporation in acknowledged trusts <u>must</u> be identified and treated separately on the corporation's balance sheets, and the Board must see to it that an appropriate officer (and counsel and the corporation's accountant) is acquainted with the terms of the relevant trust instrument.

Unless assets are held for a charitable purpose, these problems of possible trusteeship are generally of no significant concern to mutual benefit corporations. They are principally a problem for public benefit and religious corporations because the <u>somebody</u> for whom the corporate property is held may not be the party to whom the director is accountable for the performance of service.[1]

If a director is faced with an assertion that he or she, or the board as a whole, is to be held to a trusteeship standard, the matter, if involving a serious exposure, should be referred to counsel.

D. The Director With Explicit Or Implied Divided Loyalties

In certain circumstances, a board of directors may be selected by divided constituencies giving rise to special obligations.

In other situations, the corporation may seek to transfer the director's obligations to other entities.

1. The Board Reflecting Separate Constituencies

There are situations where a board of directors may be explicitly structured to provide for representation of certain interests. For example, a trade association may have a board of directors composed of men and women who are selected by separate regions or states. A university alumni association may have a board on which each of the schools of the university is represented by directors elected from the alumni of that particular school.

In such situations, a director may be faced with a conflict for which the law, as yet, provides no clear answer. The law imposes common responsibilities, powers, and duties on all directors to further the corporate mission. However, wise governance often suggests that a nonprofit board of directors be purposely structured to ensure that the views of all differing interests are heard and considered. This can create a conflict in the demands on the director. The director, in bringing to the attention of the board the particular sensitivities and concerns of his or her constituency, is aiding the whole board in the Duty of Care, and adding wisdom to the whole board's deliberations; but the Duty of Loyalty is loyalty to the corporation's overall interests, to the corporate entity itself, and not to the constituency of selection as a separate source of obligation.

The foregoing statement is perhaps a summary of the problems which a director would face if it were asserted by a special constituency that a director's actions breached a loyalty to that constituency. Judicial interpretation of this problem is virtually nonexistent.

2. Inter-Corporate Transfer Of Authority

Where allowed by state law, a corporation may contract with and empower another entity to exercise all or some of the corporation's functions and thus remove the delegating corporation's powers over those functions. The Model Act (Section 8.01) provides that to the extent that the corporate articles so provide the directors are relieved of their duties and responsibilities. The effect of such arrangements on the director's Duties of Loyalty and Care is, as yet, largely undefined and few state corporation statutes parallel the Model Act's explicit provisions relating thereto.

III DIRECTORS' RIGHTS AND SPECIAL PROBLEMS

SUGGESTED QUESTIONS AS TO
DIRECTORS' RIGHTS AND SPECIAL PROBLEMS

1.   What contact do I have with the chief executive of the corporation? Is it solely at board meetings? Should it be solely in that context?

2.   What contact do I have with subordinate staff members? Am I interfering too much?

3.   What notice is given as to board meetings? When?

4.   When do I receive the agenda and materials for board meetings? Do I have time to examine and consider them before voting thereon? Do I, in fact, read them?

5.   When do I receive minutes of prior board meetings? Do I read them? Do I see minutes or reports of committee meetings? When?

6.   Do I know of illegitimate or illegal acts of the corporation or its officers? What should I do about such acts?

7.   Was I chosen to serve on the board as a "representative" or delegate of a particular constituency? What am I expected to do for that constituency?

THE NONPROFIT CORPORATION'S CHECKLIST: CHAPTER III

Note: For purposes of simplicity in these checklists, we describe a corporation with a Chair, who presides over the Board of Directors; a Chief Executive, who may be a staff person; an Executive Committee; a Nominating Committee; and an Audit Committee. We also assume a Legal Counsel—someone, paid or unpaid, having primary responsibility for the Corporation's legal affairs. Many corporations have other Committees established for specific purposes, such as reviewing staff performance, fixing compensation, monitoring compliance with legal requirements and periodic review of bylaws. In many corporations the Executive Committee performs most or all of the functions, and these checklists will so assume.

SUBJECT	TO BE REVIEWED BY WHOM	HOW OFTEN	COMMENT
The Board's Procedures			
1. What material is distributed in advance of board meetings? Does it include:	Chair and Chief Executive	As a general matter, periodically by Chair; as to particular meetings, Chief Executive.	A regular minimum schedule of items should go out before all meetings.
a. Minutes of the last meeting?	Full Board	All regular meetings.	Always
b. Current financial statements?	Full Board, and Audit Committee	All regular meetings.	Always
c. Current reports of committees?	Full Board	At each meeting of Board	Committees should report in writing, as well as orally.
d. Summaries of decisions to be made?	Full Board	Before each meeting	All directors should be urged to study decisions before meeting: a summary is a minimum way toward this goal.

THE NONPROFIT CORPORATION'S CHECKLIST: CHAPTER III

SUBJECT	TO BE REVIEWED BY WHOM	HOW OFTEN	COMMENT
e. Copies of resolutions proposed for Adoption.	Full Board	Before each meeting	Having these resolutions distributed in advance enables the Board to focus on questions to be decided before the Board and results in increased efficiency.

ENDNOTES

1. (p. 42) The trust standard of nonprofit director conduct derives from the history of common law charitable trusts; in recent years, the corporate standard of nonprofit director conduct derived from the law of corporations has predominated in most American jurisdictions. See Olson & Hatch, Director and Officer Liability (1991) § 11.02 [1][b]; Knepper & Bailey, Liability of Corporate Officers and Directors (4th ed., 1988) § 13.04. See also discussion of exoneration statutes, infra, Chapter V.

IV

COMMITTEES

The directors of a nonprofit corporation will frequently do business through committees formed by the board. The director should understand what functions can be delegated to committees and what responsibilities the board has for their activities.

Committees are usually necessary for the efficient discharge of the board of director's business.[1] The boards of virtually all nonprofit corporations form committees for various purposes and, indeed, many of them would find it impossible to discharge their responsibilities without doing so. Nonetheless, a director should understand that there may be different types of committees depending on the purpose of the corporation and the extent to which the board delegates authority to the committee to act on behalf of the corporation. The purpose, powers and limitations of any committee should be clearly stated in the bylaws or by resolution. These documents should define the membership, term of office, and method of appointment.

A. The Types of Committees

For the purposes of this Guidebook, committees are divided into three general categories:

- Special Committees: these are temporary or ad hoc groups established for only a limited purpose.

- Standing Committees: these committees are permanent, are generally described in the bylaws and may make recommendations, oversee operations, study specific areas of activity and the like. Depending on the bylaws or resolutions creating them, they may have limited power to bind the corporation.

- Executive Committees: a committee with a general power to bind the corporation.

The above terminology is necessarily arbitrary: an infinite variety of committees is possible, but the above conceptual classifications may aid the reader in understanding the opportunities and problems in this area.

IV COMMITTEES

1.   Special Committees

Special Committees do not differ legally from agents appointed by a board of directors to perform limited functions.

Special committees can be either advisory—with no power to bind or act for the corporation—or created for a certain purpose with limited powers. The board of directors may, from time to time, create committees to investigate or recommend actions of a special nature. Those committees may be formed to buy a building, plan a reception, approve drafts of documents, make a public relations statement, or some similar purpose. They may also be asked to represent the corporation in dealing with another group or meeting. However, these committees can be delegated special powers to act as agents or to act in place of the board if the board so decides. If so, they create some of the same issues, but to a lesser extent, as executive committees as discussed below in Section 3.

Of course, a board of directors may, at any time, retain persons, entities, or organizations to investigate a problem and report to it or to serve as agents of the corporation in some matter. Thus, even the naming of a committee of total outsiders to perform some function is not outside the normal discretion of the board of directors. However, in each case the board should consider if the authority granted to such a committee is proper.

The board should note that even where a special committee has either no authority, or strictly limited authority to bind the corporation, parties outside the corporation may be entitled to rely on the apparent authority of the committee, and the committee should be warned against this danger.

2.   Standing Committees

Most nonprofit corporations find it necessary to have permanent standing committees of the board in order efficiently to discharge their business.

The board of directors may discharge their business on a particular issue through a committee created to assemble information and make recommendations concerning a particular corporate activity. The board is entitled to rely on such a committee in the normal course of business,[2] unless it has some reason to know that the committee's report is deficient.[3]

Because the work product of the committee forms part of the record of the board's action in regard to an issue, its formation, purpose and authority to act on behalf of the corporation should be clearly stated in the bylaws or in the minutes of the board meeting at which it was created. Even if the specific action taken at the meeting is simply to empower the chair to appoint the committee, and the appointment is not made until after the meeting, the purpose of the committee should also be set forth in the minutes and the chair's responsibility accordingly defined. If the committee is a permanent one, or maintained from year to year, its function should be described in the bylaws.

3. Executive Committees

Some nonprofit corporations will find that the efficient discharge of their work requires the creation of an Executive Committee able to exercise most of the power the board could exercise.

Committees empowered to bind the corporation in a wide scope of activities must, first of all, be formed consistent with the articles of incorporation and bylaws and the applicable statute creating the corporation. For an executive committee to exercise the full authority of the board, the Model Act requires that the board act in a manner consistent with the articles and bylaws (Model Act § 8.25). The exceptions to the executive committee's powers (and similar exceptions exist in most state statutes) are that the committee cannot authorize such things as the distribution of assets, dissolution or merger, the sale of substantially all the assets, or amendments or repeal of the corporate articles or bylaws.

Many nonprofit corporations find it expedient to have a single executive committee often consisting of those directors of the corporation who are also officers and a small number of other directors. The intention is to enable a committee to act for the board between its regular meetings in situations where an assembly of a quorum of the board would be impractical or impossible. Such an executive committee, in an organization of more than purely local nature, should generally consist of directors geographically close to the corporation's center of operations unless the corporation is permitted to hold committee meetings by telephone or other electronic media. (Model Act § 8.25, 8.20(c), 8.21). The board should be informed of any actions taken by the executive committee since the last meeting of the board, as promptly as is practical.

B. The Composition Of Committees

The appropriate composition of a committee will depend upon the type of committee involved. Executive committees should be composed exclusively of members of the board.

The Model Act (§ 8.25) requires that committee members be members of the board of directors. However, some state statutes permit nondirectors to serve on committees. The extent to which a committee should consist solely or predominantly of directors, or may be appointed without any directors at all, depends upon the purpose of the committee and the authority given it. In most cases at least a majority of the members of a standing committee should be directors.

As to executive committees, the membership should be exclusively of persons serving on the board of directors.

C. Procedural Issues Related To Committees

The procedures, records and operations of committees should be as clearly defined as those of the board itself.

The distinction between the board of directors' procedures and those of committees' will depend somewhat on the size of the corporation. Large nonprofit boards and their committees, such as those of national associations of various kinds, may require, for orderly or efficient procedure, a degree of formality that would be inefficient and possibly ridiculous in a small board of five or six people. The need for formality is further increased if the directors are not routinely acquainted with each other, and the board or committee meetings may be the only occasion when any interpersonal contact is achieved. In such situations, a meeting conducted according to more structured rules may be necessary. However, committees may permit a more flexible way of achieving results.

One of the principal reasons for working through committees is partly to avoid the formalities which are sometimes necessary in a board of directors' meeting—a consideration frequently observed in legislative bodies as well. Smaller groups may offer a greater openness of discussion.

Committee members are entitled to notices of meetings, quorum requirements, access to records, clear resolutions in the event of controversy, and a right to record dissent. Informality of discussions should not amount to or imply an infringement of the committee members' rights in this regard.

1. Size

As with the Board itself, committees should be selected and managed so as to maximize the efficiency of the directors in discharging their duties.

In general, smaller groups are more efficient—three to seven is an optimal size—and large committees are unwieldy. Awarding committee memberships as "perks" or to assuage egos is a sure prescription for poor performance. However, the committee must contain enough people to carry out the committee's mission and to provide representation from all whose concerns shall be examined in the committee's work. The bylaws or the resolution appointing the committee may specify the size of any committee, with particularity or by setting forth a permissible range.

2.   Committee Minutes And Records

Committees should maintain minutes of meetings and other records appropriate to their purposes. The more a board relies on a committee on a committee in the discharge of the board's duty of care, as in reliance upon the judgment and actions of an investment committee, the more a committee should be expected to maintain fully detailed minutes and records and to make regular reports to the board.

As a practical matter it may be sufficient for the board to require that a special committee prepare only a report. Standing and executive committees should submit detailed minutes to the board.

D. Indemnification And Insurance

The Indemnification and Insurance protections available to committee members should be examined along with such protections of directors generally.

As part of the management of risk of the directors of the corporation, the indemnification provisions of the articles of incorporation or bylaws should also cover committee actions. To the degree that nonboard members serve on committees, these indemnification provisions and Director's and Officer's insurance should also protect such nonboard committee members. Such coverage is not automatic, and the corporation's insurance program should be specifically reviewed to see that it exists.

E. Conflict Of Interest

The Duty of Loyalty applicable to directors is also applicable to committee service.

All standards set forth in Chapter II, regarding directors' conflicts of interest, apply to members of committees. Indeed, they apply with somewhat greater force since a conflict of a single member of a small committee directly affects whether a nonmember director not serving on the committee may reasonably believe the committee's recommendations merit confidence.

IV COMMITTEES

F. Specific Committees

The board of directors should, from time to time, create various committees and define their functions as the efficient discharge of its duties requires. However, it should specifically examine the possible need for a nominating committee and an audit committee.

Most standing and special committees will be created as the need arises, and include committees such as Personnel or Human Resources, Planning, Public Relations, Finance, Programming, Capital Campaigns and Grants. However, the nominating and audit committees need special attention and are recommended for all nonprofit corporations. A compensation committee should also be considered. In any event, whether a separate committee is formed for this function or it is assigned to another body within the board, the corporation should clearly organize the review of staff qualifications and compensation, and, in particular, the compensation of the Chief Executive. Since such a task involves the receipt and evaluation of confidential and sensitive data, it should be assigned to a separate standing committee where the board resources are large enough to make this possible.

To the extent possible, such compensation should be related to performance in meeting annual goals. The entire board should be aware of and approve the total compensation package.

1. Nominating Committees

Good corporate practice suggests the appointment of a nominating committee in order to strengthen the corporate mission.

A nominating committee is almost always a standing committee and is rarely regarded as a body whose diligence or negligence is legally reviewed. Yet, even if the corporation has no legal obligations[4] to others concerning the choice of its directors or officers, the process of this choice may seriously alter the corporation's future.

The corporate mission may require racial and gender diversification in the corporation's controlling bodies, or such diversity may be necessary in order to be considered for government and other funds. Such requirements emphasize the need for an active nominating committee, but even apart from such specific demands the nominating committee should formalize and develop procedures for determining who should have positions on the board itself and on committees. The presence of a nominating committee also helps to ensure that important board decisions regarding the appointment of directors, management, and committee members will not be handled on a default basis by management alone.

IV COMMITTEES

The nominating committee may also have responsibility for recommending removal of a director in the unusual circumstances when removal is appropriate, prior to the expiration of a director's term of office. It may also have broader-ranging functions, such as determining the optimum size of the board over a period of time, whether or not particular management members should serve on the board, the types and functions of board committees, the retention or removal of the chief executive, board operations, including the quality and timeliness of information to the board, the qualifications of membership on each committee, and the evaluation of likely successors to management positions.[5] Such review should include the board profile as to age, gender, racial balance, etc.

Ideally, the Nominating Committee should be composed of directors who do not participate in management and are free of relationships, both business and personal, which will interfere with their exercise of independent judgment. This will help provide both the appearance and the reality of objectivity. In addition, it may, in some situations, be prudent to rotate the members of the committee. A compromise should be reached between the need to draw on the corporation's present activities, history and experience, and the need for fresh insights into the corporation's present and future mission.

2.   Audit Committee

Good corporate practice suggests the need of a committee to review and guide accounting and audit practices. Such a committee should be comprised solely of directors.

An audit committee has responsibilities concerning the corporation's auditing, accounting and control functions. In fulfilling these functions, for all but the very small corporations, an outside accountant should be retained to review and opine or comment on the corporation's books and records. Federal and state laws or regulation may require a formal audit by a certified public accountant. In order to retain objectivity of the audit process, employees of the corporation, even if serving on the board of directors, should not be members of the audit committee.

The committee's duties usually include choosing services needed, reviewing reports and determining adequate procedures and controls, reviewing financial performance and approving the annual budget for submission to the board. Sometimes a review of legal compliance is included within the duties of an audit committee. Any additional duties should be undertaken with caution, for if the committee becomes involved in operational matters, it may jeopardize its essential independence from management. In order to adhere to the proper limits, the duties delegated to the committee should be spelled out very specifically, after consultation with and the concurrence of the outside accountant. This definition of duties can be accomplished either by bylaw or by board resolution.

IV COMMITTEES

SUGGESTED QUESTIONS AS TO COMMITTEES

1.   What committees does our Board have? What powers does each committee have?

2.   Is there an executive committee? What are the limitations on its power to act?

3.   Who monitors the corporation's accounting and financial reports? Is there an audit committee? Who serves on it?

4.   Is there a committee which reviews staff performance and compensation?

5.   How do committees report to the board?

6.   Am I permitted, encouraged, forbidden or discouraged from attending meetings of committees of which I am not a member?

7.   Do we have a nominating committee?

8.   Does the nominating committee review the board profile as to age, gender, racial balance, etc.?

THE NONPROFIT CORPORATION'S CHECKLIST: CHAPTER IV

Note: For purposes of simplicity in these checklists, we describe a corporation with a Chair, who presides over the Board of Directors; a Chief Executive, who may be a staff person; an Executive Committee; a Nominating Committee; and an Audit Committee. We also assume a Legal Counsel—someone, paid or unpaid, having primary responsibility for the Corporation's legal affairs. Many corporations have other Committees established for specific purposes, such as reviewing staff performance, fixing compensation, monitoring compliance with legal requirements and periodic review of bylaws. In many corporations the Executive Committee performs most or all of the functions, and these checklists will so assume.

SUBJECT	TO BE REVIEWED BY WHOM	HOW OFTEN	COMMENT
Committees			
What are the committees of the corporation?	Chair, Chief Executive, full Board	Annually	A review of bylaw provisions relating to committees should be performed simultaneously.
a. Which of them have power to bind the corporation?	Chair, Chief Executive, full Board	Annually	A review of bylaw provisions relating to committees should be performed simultaneously.
b. Which of them, with or without power to bind the corporation, deals with major parties or interests outside the corporation?	Chair, Chief Executive, full Board	Annually	A review of bylaw provisions relating to committees should be performed simultaneously.
c. Which committees simply report or advise the board?	Chair, Chief Executive, full Board	Annually	A review of bylaw provisions relating to committees should be performed simultaneously.

THE NONPROFIT CORPORATION'S CHECKLIST: CHAPTER IV

SUBJECT	TO BE REVIEWED BY WHOM	HOW OFTEN	COMMENT
d. Do we have a Nominating Committee?	Chair, Chief Executive, full Board	Annually, in preparation for annual meeting; before each meeting at which a vacancy is to be filled.	An effective nominating committee must discuss board evaluation and board needs with full board prior to annual meeting.
e. Should there be provisions limiting the number of consecutive terms a director may serve? Or a maximum age for directors?	Nominating Committee, reviewing proposed changes with Legal Counsel, and reporting to Board	Probably every three or four years	Nominating Committee should, as a regular function, analyze years of service of each director, maximum age, and average age of board. No clear choices are implied; but decisions on these issues (including the decision to make no changes) should be conscious.
f. Should there be a board having staggered terms, so one-half or one-third of the board is chosen each year?	Nominating Committee, reviewing proposed changes with Legal Counsel, and reporting to Board	Probably every three or four years	Again, a periodic review should lead to a decision of change or continuation of existing procedures.
g. What committee reviews staff compensation?	Chair, Chief Executive, full Board	Annually	This function should be formally assigned even if no separate Compensation Committee is created.
h. Does that committee report to the Board in executive session?	Chair, Chief Executive, full Board	Annually	Discussion of staff salaries should always be held outside of the presence of staff, without need for a special resolution to that effect.

ENDNOTES

1. (p. 48) See Kurtz, <u>Board Liability</u> (1988) pp. 10-13.

2. (p. 49) <u>Model Act</u> § 8.30(b).

3. (p. 49) <u>Model Act</u> § 8.25 Comment. See Chapter II, Section 2 on Reliance.

4. (p. 53) Some statutes specifically provide for a nominating committee; see Pa. C.S.A. (Purdon, 1991) § 5725(e).

5. (p. 54) A good general guide to this process is Nelson, <u>Six Keys to Recruiting, Orienting and Involving Nonprofit Board Members</u>, (National Center for Nonprofit Boards, Washington, D.C. 1991).

V

THE DIRECTOR'S RISK AND PROTECTION AGAINST IT

The director's potential liability to third parties, or to the corporation, and the available protections against this exposure require separate scrutiny by the director.

In the last several years, there has been an increase of litigation against directors of some nonprofit corporations. The demise of the charitable immunity exemption[1] has increased the frequency of suits against directors and officers of public benefit and religious corporations. Mutual benefit corporations and their directors have never enjoyed the protection of the charitable exemption. Although many small nonprofit corporation boards face little or no practical risk, all directors need to understand the actions which may be taken for their protection.

The director should, before accepting office, understand what the corporation's basic documents provide as to indemnification and insurance and identify any statutory exoneration or other legal provisions which may limit the director's liability.

1. The Director's Exposure

A director's possible liability in litigation does not arise simply because the corporation may be liable; it arises because the director is charged with some breach of duty owed either to the corporation or to a specific party. A director should understand that the corporation itself may be the party asserting a claim.

A director's liability does not automatically arise from corporate liability. Directors, to be endangered by litigation, actual or threatened, must hold a duty to some party entitled—or allegedly entitled—to sue in enforcement thereof. Suits against directors are typically brought in one of three ways.

First, an outside party may attempt to sue a member of the board directly alleging some injury by the corporation itself, joining the director as some kind of principal or implied co-conspirator.

Second, an aggrieved party may assert some right of the corporation against the director, suing to enforce an alleged right of the corporation; law suits of this type are referred to as "derivative actions". In effect, the corporation is suing the director to enforce the corporation's rights, generally because of the director's breach of the Duty of Care or the Duty of Loyalty.

V THE DIRECTORS' RISK AND PROTECTION AGAINST IT

Third, the director may be held independently liable under various statutory provisions dealing with issues such as environmental claims, tax delinquencies (for example, sales taxes), and antitrust claims.

The exposure here will vary greatly from small charitable entities, which may confer little vulnerability, to large trade associations. The exposure will be determined more by the type of nonprofit corporation in question than by its size. Generally exposure here is based on allegations of negligence or failure to oversee.

2. Avoidance Of Risk

Directors May Avoid Some Risks by Reorganization of Decision Making.

Some directors may wish to employ advisers and consultants to aid in decisions. In some cases, the use of outside contractors is obviously cosmetic and an expensive and perhaps fruitless attempt to evade responsibility and the exposure to risk which responsibility brings. But in some circumstances the Duty of Care may be more fully demonstrated by seeking independent advice and, in situations where the Duty of Loyalty presents problems, the use of an outside opinion, even to verify the obvious, may be prudent.

3. Indemnification

The director should seek a program of corporate indemnification to the maximum extent permitted by applicable corporation law. Such a program of indemnification should be sought even if the corporation's liquid net worth may make such protection limited in value.

Although the value of indemnification depends on both the legal and financial ability of the corporation to pay, the legal right of the corporation to indemnify depends on the type of loss the director has incurred. In some instances the corporation is required to indemnify while in others the indemnification is permitted if the corporation so chooses. A corporation may also advance certain litigation expenses to the director in certain circumstances.

a. Discretionary Indemnification

Initially it should be noted that even if the board of directors wants to indemnify another director, such indemnification must be consistent with state statutes and the corporation's by-laws and articles. Mere goodwill of the board is not sufficient to authorize indemnification.

V THE DIRECTORS' RISK AND PROTECTION AGAINST IT

The Model Act (§ 8.51) gives the corporation discretion to indemnify the director if the director has acted in good faith and with the reasonable belief that his or her actions were in the best interests of the corporation. Such indemnification may include sums due under a settlement agreement. Indemnification for proceedings by the corporation against the director (whether direct or derivative) is limited to the reasonable expenses incurred by the director in connection with the proceedings. Model Act (§ 8.51(e)). Such discretionary indemnification may be made mandatory by appropriate provisions in the Articles of Incorporation and the bylaws.

b.   Mandatory Indemnification

We must now analyze the director's _right_ to indemnification from the corporation. We shall use the Model Act as a guide here. Individual state statutes may differ from the Model Act, but the issues treated by the Model Act are ones which the director must face in any event. Under the Model Act (§ 8.52), a corporation is required to indemnify a director for "reasonable expenses" if the director is wholly successful in his or her defense of any proceeding of which the director is a party as a result of being a director of the corporation.

Nonetheless, the director should endeavor to have corporate indemnification to the fullest extent permitted by applicable law. This means that the corporate obligation should be set forth in the Articles of Incorporation, in as broad language as the applicable statute permits. Each director may wish to have a separate contract with the corporation providing for such indemnification.

The director must recognize that the corporation's uninsured obligation to indemnify may be of little use to the director, if the corporation's net worth is insufficient to cover the director's expense or the director's exposure.

c.   Advances Of Expenses

A director will wish to know that specific measures have been adopted by the corporation to provide for as much advances for legal expenses as is permitted. The Model Act (8.53) sets forth the conditions upon which such advances may be made. A nonprofit corporation may advance expenses to a director if:

First, the director furnishes a written affirmation of the director's good faith belief that the standard of conduct permitting indemnification has been met.

Second, the director furnishes a written undertaking to repay any sums advanced if it is ultimately determined that the director did not meet the applicable standard.

Third, a determination is made that the facts known to whomever makes the determination would not preclude indemnity.

These requirements are not onerous and are in the interest of both the corporation and the director. Indemnification—which takes place only at the end of litigation—is of limited help to the director, without an advance for expenses. As noted above, directors should demand that the corporate documents require the maximum protection which the applicable corporation statute will permit.

d.   Third Party Indemnification

In addition, indemnification for directors may be sought from any third party who may be agreeing to indemnify the corporation on a related matter. The director should learn whether such third party indemnification can run directly to a director, or runs only to the corporation. The director should further ascertain at what point this protection becomes available.

4. Protection Of Directors Through Insurance

A nonprofit corporation should obtain insurance to protect its directors and officers.

A director's and officer's insurance policy ("D&O insurance") may, subject to the applicable corporation act, provide coverage that is broader than any indemnification permitted by the Model Act or by relevant state law. Under the Model Act (Section 8.57), a corporation can protect a director by insurance, even if the insurance coverage extends protection to situations in which the corporation otherwise could not indemnify. Some state statutes prohibit indemnification against settlements and judgments in derivative actions (i.e., lawsuits asserting the corporation's rights against the director), if a director is adjudged liable, unless the court determines that special circumstances entitle the director to indemnity despite that judgment. And even where such special indemnification is allowed, few statutes permit corporations to indemnify the director against all claims, expenses and fines.[2] In contrast, most corporation statutes permit the corporation to procure insurance for the director for such events even though the corporation could not indemnify.

V THE DIRECTORS' RISK AND PROTECTION AGAINST IT

a.   Why Purchase D&O Insurance?

A director should expect the corporation to provide D&O insurance protecting him or her from liability and, where such insurance is not provided, examine the risks of serving without it.

As previously discussed, even if a nonprofit corporation has expansive indemnification provisions in its articles of incorporation or bylaws,[3] these assurances must be considered in light of the financial strength of the corporation offering them. To the extent that qualified board members may be deterred from participating because of inadequate financial reserves to pay such claims, D&O insurance may be the most viable method of providing both the perception and reality of adequate protection for board members—current and prospective. No director should serve without insurance if meaningful insurance would be available to the corporation at reasonable cost.[4]

b.   A D&O Policy Should Be Reviewed To Determine Whether And How The Coverage Varies With The Role Played By An Individual Who Is A Director In Each Of His Or Her Capacities.

A corporation should refer to its articles of incorporation, bylaws and board minutes to determine who is an officer or director. If an individual is playing two or more roles, the insurance coverage may be determined by what role is engaged in at the time of the action. Where a corporation has affiliates or subsidiaries, the extension of the insurance coverage to these entities should be verified. Newly created subsidiaries and the election of directors and officers after the commencement of the policy may also require changes to the policy.

The policy should also be examined to determine if it covers the activities of non-director members of committees.

c.   D&O Coverage May Be Affected By Dual Roles of a Director and Other Insurance Coverage of a Director

Many typical D&O policies do not cover the activities of a director or officer when she or he is acting in other capacities. For example, when a board member who is an attorney is acting in the capacity of counsel, whether paid or volunteer, his or her conduct is probably not included in the corporation's D&O protection. Such dual roles can give rise to difficult questions concerning coverage. Legal malpractice insurers may specifically exclude claims which arise if the attorney was acting as an officer or director of an organization. The typical D&O policy may have a similar provision excluding work performed as a lawyer unless the attorney is specifically named in the policy. Thus, there may be a gray area in which neither coverage may apply, especially if the attorney or her or his law firm is also legal counsel to the corporation.[5] Similar problems can arise in other dual roles. These problems may yield to special riders or endorsements on policies; but the need for clarification should be recognized.

d.   The Nature Of "Claims Made" Policies

Most D&O policies are written on a "claims made" basis and thus it would be appropriate for the director to understand the limits of this type of coverage.

Policy coverage on a "claims made" basis means that a claim is covered by insurance only if the policy is in effect at the time that the claim is made, regardless of when the event causing the claim occurred. Furthermore, some D&O policies will limit the coverage of prior events to those arising in a few years prior to the inception of the policy.

The "claims made" type of policy contrasts with an "occurrence" policy. Occurrence policies cover all claims arising out of incidents occurring during the policy period, regardless of whether the insurance policy is still in effect at the time the claim is made. Most insurance policies with which a director will be individually familiar—e.g., automobile liability, fire and extended coverage—are "occurrence" policies. As can be seen, "claims made" coverage may offer a very limited protection. Such policies typically require the corporation to advise the insurer promptly of facts that could trigger claims, and delicate issues arise as to what constitutes notice of a claim. The director should further understand that if the corporation discontinues a D&O policy after she or he ceases to be a director, the director may be uninsured even as to acts occurring during the director's term of office, if the claim is made after the policy is discontinued.

e.   Policy Coverage

A D&O policy typically consists of one part covering the director and one part providing reimbursement of the corporation for sums paid or payable by it to the director.

D&O policies are typically divided into two parts. The first part covers reimbursement of individual directors and officers for losses for which they are not indemnified by the corporation. The second part provides reimbursement to the corporation for amounts which it has paid, or is required to expend, in indemnifying its directors and officers.[6] In other words, it provides the funds which enable the corporation to discharge its obligation to indemnify.

V THE DIRECTORS' RISK AND PROTECTION AGAINST IT

The type of coverage, retentions, exclusions and other aspects of the policies are sufficiently complex as to require study by the corporation's insurance committee, any insurance consultant, possibly by legal counsel. The issues should be reviewed whenever insurance carriers are changed.

f.   What Losses Are Covered?

The D&O policy should be analyzed to determine whether the duty to defend and the cost of defense are covered. The corporation should provide the director with a memorandum on this subject as well as the losses covered or not covered. Usually, for example, there is no duty to provide attorneys to defend a lawsuit, nor do typical D&O policies provide for the payment of legal expenses, except after a final determination of liability under the policy.[7] Thus, technically, a D&O policy is an indemnity policy, as distinguished from a liability policy.

Under an indemnity policy, such as the typical D&O policy, the insurer is not required to make any payments until the insured has suffered an actual loss (i.e. has been required to make a payment). A liability insurance policy, such as the typical automobile insurance policy, requires the insurer to make certain payments even though the insured has not yet lost or paid any out-of-pocket money.[8] It is because of the nature of a D&O policy that the advances for expenses mentioned above is so crucial for the director's protection.

A director will also want to know:

- The limits of coverage of the D&O policy (i.e. the highest amount of money the insurer will pay for each loss). This will be affected by any offset of legal defense costs;

- The retention level imposed on the insureds, more commonly known as the "deductible" (i.e. how much of the loss must be borne by the director before the insurer will begin to provide payment for the loss); and

- The amount of co-insurance, if any (i.e., the percentage that the insured continues to be responsible for paying, even when deductibles have been satisfied and the insurance is providing coverage for a loss).

V THE DIRECTORS' RISK AND PROTECTION AGAINST IT

g.   Policy Exclusions

Virtually all D&O policies have substantial exclusions which must be fully understood.

Perhaps more important than the scope of coverage, most D&O policies are riddled with exclusions. The excluded risks are not just limited to the "exclusions section" itself but occur throughout the policies. For example the term "loss" may be defined to exclude fines or penalties imposed by law for matters uninsurable under applicable law such as punitive damages. Other definitions and terms also set forth exclusions.[9]

The standard exclusions often involve some types of risks which could produce sizable claims against directors and officers. Often excluded are the following liabilities: losses covered by other insurance; miscellaneous exposures such as sickness or death resulting from pollution; ERISA claims; fair employment claims; libel or slander actions; and liabilities arising from intentional conduct, including fraud, dishonesty and criminal conduct. .Most policies will not cover fines, penalties, or punitive damages.

Many of the exclusions may be deleted by negotiation and payment of a separate premium. A few specialized exposures (such as ERISA claims) may be covered by specific policies. While such a request may constitute the "red-flagging" of a problem, the disclosure of potential claims is already required in the application.

h.   The Application

All Applications For D&O Insurance Should Be Carefully Prepared And Reviewed.

The application for D&O insurance and the statements made in it are part of the insurance contract and may be relied upon by the insurer when an issue is raised as to the policy's coverage. Because of the peculiar importance of D&O insurance, all directors should be sure that not only the policy itself, but also the application for it, have been reviewed with particular care since a misstatement in the application (even if the director is unaware of it) may result in a denial of coverage.

V THE DIRECTORS' RISK AND PROTECTION AGAINST IT

5. Statutory Protections For Directors

Many state statutes limit the liability of a nonprofit director.

As a partial response to the increased exposure of directors, and the possible unavailability of insurance, more than one-half of the states have amended their nonprofit corporation statutes to limit a director's liability to special situations involving such things as gross negligence or wilful malfeasance. Such is the intent of Section 8.30(d) of the Model Act. Some such statutes apply only to public benefit corporations. A director should nonetheless note that the expense of establishing due care and good faith, even if the director is successful in doing so, can be significant and indemnification, insured if possible, is still to be desired.[10]

Some statutes may require that the corporation amend the Articles of Incorporation to make these provisions applicable. Directors should make sure that all actions needed to make this protection available have been taken.

Furthermore, the director should be aware of two fundamental weaknesses in such statutes. First of all, many plaintiffs will predictably assert in the initial complaint that the act or omission involved <u>was</u> grossly negligent or wilful: that is, the director may still have defend himself or herself in a court proceeding. Hence, again the need for advances of expenses. Second, the impact of these state statutes on causes of action arising under federal law is, as of this writing, unknown.

Other statutes limit certain types of claims. For example there have been attempts to place limits on professional liability claims against hospitals and physicians in many states.[11]

6. The Director and Legal Counsel

The director should recognize:

> a) The legal positions of the board of directors and that of the corporation are not <u>necessarily</u> identical: in some situations the board or a portion thereof needs to seek counsel of its own, since the corporate general counsel may be obligated to pursue or assert claims against the directors. The conduct of the director and that of the corporation and its officers may be materially different.

> b) An individual director may, in extreme situations, need independent counsel if such director finds that his or her

situation differs markedly from that of other members of the board.

In general, the board of directors is the highest authority of the corporation, and, as to matters concerning the entire board, the corporation and the board are roughly identical in their legal exposure. But, in some instances, the board may have a conflicting interest. If the corporation and the board are both defendants in a proceeding, the corporation may wish to assert, or be forced to assert, cross claims against the board.

Furthermore, individual directors may, through their own acts or omissions, find themselves separated from the rest of the board in some contested transaction.

V THE DIRECTORS' RISK AND PROTECTION AGAINST IT

SUGGESTED QUESTIONS AS TO THE
DIRECTOR'S RISK AND PROTECTION AGAINST IT

1.   What exposure do I have to claims or litigation brought against me? Claims asserted by whom? Claims asserted for what reason?

2.   Have the directors of the corporation, past or present, been subject to such litigation or threats of it? Why? With what result?

3.   Do I know of a similar corporation where the directors have been sued?

4.   What provisions do the corporate articles and bylaws have with regard to the director's risk, indemnification and insurance?

5.   Of those provisions, which ones are mandatory ones which I can insist upon, and which require some approval or ratification? By whom? According to what standard?

6.   Do the mandatory provisions include the advance of expenses?

7.   Do I know what our corporation's D&O policy provides? What is not covered by it?

8.   What is the earliest event which is covered even if a claim comes within the policy period?

9.   Who has read or examined the corporation's D&O Policy?

10.   Have I been provided with a memorandum describing our D&O coverage, available indemnification, and statutory protections available?

11.   Have I been informed as to the interrelationship of the corporation's D&O coverage and other policies insuring me, such as professional malpractice, or umbrella liability policies? Are there gaps in my protection here?

12.   If I cease to be a director, for how long a period, if any, will the corporation's D&O policy cover me?

13.   If I have D&O coverage supplied in connection with another corporation, does it cover me as a director of this nonprofit corporation?

14.   Do applicable statutes limit my liability or exonerate me? Has the corporation taken all steps necessary to make those limitations or exonerations effective?

THE NONPROFIT CORPORATION'S CHECKLIST: CHAPTER V

Note: For purposes of simplicity in these checklists, we describe a corporation with a Chair, who presides over the Board of Directors; a Chief Executive, who may be a staff person; an Executive Committee; a Nominating Committee; and an Audit Committee. We also assume a Legal Counsel—someone, paid or unpaid, having primary responsibility for the Corporation's legal affairs. Many corporations have other Committees established for specific purposes, such as reviewing staff performance, fixing compensation, monitoring compliance with legal requirements and periodic review of bylaws. In many corporations the Executive Committee performs most or all of the functions, and these checklists will so assume.

SUBJECT	TO BE REVIEWED BY WHOM	HOW OFTEN	COMMENT
The Director's Risk			
1. Do we have D&O insurance? What events does it cover?	Legal Counsel: Prospective Board members	At least annually; at each change in Board; at each change of insurer or alteration in policy coverage	
a. As defined by the date of occurrence of the event?	Legal Counsel	At least annually	This is not just an analysis of dates of policy itself, but analysis of how far it covers prior events.
b. As defined by the date on which a claim under the policy is made?	Legal Counsel	At least annually	This requires the board to understand what event constitutes a claim, and the nature of a claims made policy. A memorandum to the directors should cover this issue.

THE NONPROFIT CORPORATION'S CHECKLIST: CHAPTER V

SUBJECT	TO BE REVIEWED BY WHOM	HOW OFTEN	COMMENT
c. In terms of what events are not covered?	Legal Counsel	At least annually	This requires the board to understand what event constitutes a claim, or an insurable event, and what events are not covered. A memorandum to the directors should cover this issue.
d. What are the deductibles? What co-insurance is required?	Legal Counsel	At least annually	This requires the board to understand what event constitutes a claim, or an insurable event, and what events are not covered. A memorandum to the directors should cover this issue.
2. Does our D&O policy exclude coverage where an otherwise insured person is covered by another liability policy — e.g., an attorney's malpractice policy?	Legal Counsel	At least annually	Directors having dual coverage should inform Audit Committee and Counsel.
3. If so, have we reviewed how possible gaps in coverage can be plugged?	Legal Counsel, any Board member having dual coverage	At least annually	Larger corporations may use professional risk consultants in this task.

ENDNOTES

1. (p. 59) Until a few years ago, many states held that charities were immune from lawsuits arising from injuries caused by employees or agents. This immunity has virtually disappeared, through legislation and judicial decision.

2. (p. 62) Knepper & Bailey, Liability of Corporate Officers and Directors (4th Ed. 1988), at ch. 21. Model Act (§ 8.43); Arsht, Indemnification Under Section 145 of the Delaware General Corporation Law, 3 Del. J. Corp. L. 176-177 (1978).

3. (p. 63) See Frederick, Indemnification & Liability of Corporate Directors and Officers, J. of Mo. B. (July-August 1987) regarding the provision of additional indemnity pursuant to Mo. Rev. Stat. § 351.355(7) (1986). Since this Missouri statute requires shareholder approval for additional indemnity provisions that are contained in a corporation's bylaws or a separate agreement, many practitioners have advised that, in the case of nonprofit corporations, any additional indemnity provision must be included in the entity's articles of incorporation in order to comply with the statute.

4. (p. 63) For more information on this topic, see Edie, Directors and Officers Liability Insurance and Indemnification (Council on Foundations, Washington, D.C. 1988); Tremper, D & O—Yes or No?: Insurance for the Volunteer Board (National Center for Community Risk Management & Insurance, Washington, D.C. 1992).

    Although some corporate general liability and individual personal liability policies will cover an individual's service as a director, such coverage is rarely complete. In times past, some homeowners' policies contained coverage for specific nonprofit civic activities of the insured. These provisions have largely been eliminated and were narrowly defined at best.

5. (p. 64) See D. Stern, Avoiding Legal Malpractice Claims, J. of Mo. B., 263 (June 1988).

6. (p. 64) Knepper & Bailey, Liability of Corporate Officers and Directors (4th ed. 1988) 835 et seq. (appendix C). See also Goldwasser, Dan L., Practicing Law Institute, Directors' and Officers' Liability Insurance 1988, 325 (1988).

7. (p. 65) Zaborac v. American Casualty Co., 663 F. Supp. 330 (C.D. Ill. 1987). But see Okada v. MGIC Indemnity Corporation, 823 F.2d 276 (9th Cir. 1987) which held to the contrary. There is considerable dispute among courts as to when legal fees would be payable. Some courts require legal fees to be paid as they are billed and payable. Pepsico, Inc. v. Continental Casualty Corp., 640 F. Supp. 656 (S.D. N.Y.

1986). Insurers are modifying policy language to make concurrent payment obtainable. Goldwasser, <u>supra</u> note 7, at 173.

8. (p. 65) In addition, an insured can be liable for legal defense costs as well as for damages on the claim itself when they exceed policy limits. And, a large deductible can subject a corporate insured to paying a significant portion of the initial defense costs. Goldwasser, <u>supra</u>, note 7 at 66-7 and 457. Thus, many nonprofit corporations may be underinsured.

9. (p. 66) Knepper & Bailey, <u>Liability of Corporate Officers and Directors</u> (4th ed. 1988)

10. (p. 67) Laws limiting the liability of nonprofit organizations' directors and officers are digested in <u>State Liability Laws for Charitable Organizations and Volunteers</u> (National Center for Community Risk Management & Insurance, Washington, D.C. 1992). Olson & Hatch, <u>Director and Officer Liability</u> (1991) § 11.03. For a critical view of one such statute, (p. 98) See Harrison & Marhoun, <u>Protection for Unpaid Directors and Officers of Illinois Not-For-Profits: Fact or Fiction</u>? 79 Ill. Bar J. 172 (April 1991), and a critique of the latter article, 79 Ill. Bar J. 267 (June 1991).

11. (p. 67) A general survey of this problem is <u>State Liability Laws for Charitable Organizations and Volunteers</u> (Nonprofits' Risk Management & Insurance Institute, Washington, D.C., 1990).

VI

TAXATION

A director should understand the basic application of federal and local tax law to the corporation.

A director should have a general understanding of the tax status of the corporation. The director should know, for example: if the corporation is exempt from federal income tax; if the corporation is exempt from local real estate or other taxes; and, in a general way, what is required to maintain such exemptions.

Taxation is a technical field, and a director's obligations do not require a detailed knowledge of the various tax statutes and regulations. Most nonprofit corporations have, or should consider having, their tax reporting handled by outside professionals, either accountants or attorneys. The function of the board, in oversight of these persons, is part of the oversight which the board exercises generally.

The subject is a broad one, but this chapter will outline only the principal federal income tax issues of the more common nonprofit corporations.[1] And, despite the importance of local tax issues, we do not address state and local tax law: space constrains us. However, directors must understand that federal tax-exempt status does not automatically confer exemption from state and local taxes.[2]

1. Qualifying For Exemption From Federal Income Tax

Most nonprofit corporations are exempt from the federal income taxes applicable to corporations. However, corporations do not automatically qualify for exemption from federal income taxation simply because they are nonprofit.

A director should not assume that because the corporation is nonprofit it is exempt from any income tax whatsoever. Tax exempt status is a privilege, not a right, that is conferred on an organization which meets and continues to meet certain requirements set out by the Internal Revenue Code (Code). Organizations seeking exemption under Section 501(C)(3), described in this chapter, must obtain IRS approval of their applications for exemption. The Internal Revenue Service (IRS) lists 27 types of tax-exempt organizations in IRS Publication 557, Tax-Exempt Status for Your Organization, along with brief descriptions defining their activities.[3] This list is set forth in Appendix B of this Guidebook.

A director should understand that exemption from federal income tax does not necessarily permit donors to the corporation to deduct gifts to it. Tax exemption of the corporation permits deduction of gifts to the corporation only if the corporation qualifies under Code § 501(c)(3). Payments to other types of tax-exempt corporations may be deductible by the donor only if the payment qualifies as a trade or business expense.

VI TAXATION

2. Corporations Exempt From Tax Under § 501(c)(3)

Most public benefit and religious corporations, and any such corporation wishing deductibility of gifts as charitable contributions, will seek exemption under Code § 501(c)(3).

For a corporation to be exempt under § 501(c)(3) it must be organized and operated for a charitable purpose.

A nonprofit corporation may qualify for exemption from federal income tax as a § 501(c)(3) organization if it is organized and operated exclusively for charitable, religious, educational, literary or scientific purposes.[4] These general categories conform roughly to the traditional trust and corporate law definitions of "charity".

a. Particular Advantages Of 501(c)(3) Status

In addition to exemption of the corporation itself from most federal income taxes, § 501(c)(3) organizations enjoy certain unique advantages. Contributions made to them are tax-deductible by the contributors, up to the limits imposed by Code § 170(b).[5] In addition, some § 501(c)(3) corporations may finance their exempt activities by issuing tax-exempt bonds, enabling these organizations to lower their borrowing costs.

b. General Requirements

To achieve and maintain exemption under § 501(c)(3) the corporation must comply with explicit restrictions.

In order to be tax exempt under § 501(c)(3) a corporation must conduct the qualifying functions referred to above, and it must be: organized and operated exclusively for exempt purposes; must not have any earnings inure to private individuals; it must not carry on substantial activities to influence legislation; and it must not participate, in any way, in any political campaign.[6] Furthermore, with limited exception the IRS must approve an application for such exemption, as described in more detail in Section 6 below.

The requirement that the corporation be organized exclusively for exempt purposes, means that the articles of incorporation (and any amendments thereto) must contain appropriate restrictions on the corporation's purposes, activities and use of assets, including ultimate disposition of assets upon a dissolution of the corporation. A director should bear this in mind in considering any amendments to the articles. It is not sufficient that the corporation merely operate in an appropriate manner.

c. Limitations On Unrelated Business Activities

The conduct of unrelated business activities may not disqualify an otherwise exempt § 501(c)(3) corporation if the amount of activity is insubstantial: however, the corporation may be taxed on income from the unrelated activity.

A § 501(c)(3) corporation may engage in some activities that are not related to its exempt purposes. For example, the corporation may own property which it leases to commercial tenants when the property is not needed by the corporation. Such activities will not disqualify the corporation from tax-exempt status so long as the corporation's unrelated activities are not a <u>substantial</u> part of the corporation's overall activities.

Income derived from certain unrelated activities may be subject to federal tax. See the discussion of Unrelated Business Income in Section 7.

d. Limitations On Private Benefit And Private Inurement

The activities of a § 501(c)(3) corporation must not be for the benefit of a shareholder or individual.

A § 501(c)(3) corporation is not operated for charitable purposes if it serves a private interest. This is the general standard applicable to all charitable corporations and simply incorporates into the Code the trust law standards of a charity. Further, in order for the corporation to be recognized as a § 501(c)(3) organization "no part of the net earnings of" a corporation may inure "to the benefit of the private shareholder or individual." Private benefit or private inurement may occur when a § 501(c)(3) corporation pays for goods or services in sums in excess of their fair market value or when assets of a corporation are given to or used for the benefit of an individual who gave less than fair consideration for the same.

VI TAXATION

e. **Limitations On Lobbying**

A corporation will not qualify as a § 501(c)(3) organization if it devotes a substantial part of its activities to lobbying, propaganda or attempting to influence legislation.

§ 501(h) of the Code provides a safe harbor for certain corporations that wish to regularly engage in some lobbying. Although § 501(h) clarifies the scope of permitted activities, it can impose strict penalties on the corporation and its directors if these safe harbor limits are exceeded.

As a general rule, a corporation will not be considered to be engaging in substantial lobbying if less than five percent of its activities are devoted to such activity.

Certain qualifying organizations may file a special election to allow them to spend a specified dollar amount (which may represent a larger percentage) for lobbying. Persistent lobbying in excess of that permitted by § 501(h) will lead to a loss of not only the protection of the § 501(h) safe harbor but also a loss of the corporation's basic tax exemption. In addition, penalty taxes may be imposed on any officer, director, or responsible employee of the organization involved.

f. **The Absolute Prohibition On Political Campaign Activities**

A § 501(c)(3) corporation cannot participate or intervene in any political campaign.

A § 501(c)(3) corporation will lose its tax-exempt status if it participates or intervenes in a political campaign on behalf of, or in opposition to, a candidate for public office, and it will be subject to an excise tax of 10 percent of such political expenditures. Unlike the restrictions on lobbying, the prohibition on political activities is absolute, and applies to any such activities, no matter how small. There are severe penalties imposed on the corporation and, in some instances, its directors, if prohibited political activities continue.[7]

VI TAXATION

3. Special Rules Relating To § 501(c)(3) Corporations — Public Charities And Private Foundations

All 501(c)(3) corporation are regarded as private foundations unless they demonstrate that their activities or the nature of their financial support conform to certain defined exceptions. Private foundations are subject to various restrictions and possible taxes not applicable to other 501(c)(3) corporations.

The Code classifies certain § 501(c)(3) organizations as "private foundations," in contrast to "public charities," the latter being the term commonly used to refer to those § 501(c)(3) organizations that are not private foundations, although this term does not appear in the Code. A director should understand that any § 501(c)(3) corporation will be treated as a private foundation <u>unless</u> it can demonstrate that it meets one of the definitions of a public charity, as described below. Since private foundations are subject to greater restrictions and some taxes not applicable to public charities, a § 501(c)(3) corporation should make sure that the classification of the organization as a public charity or private foundation is properly determined and maintained. This Guidebook gives this question only a brief survey.

a. Definition Of Public Charity

A corporation can avoid the additional taxes and restrictions imposed on private foundations if it falls within one of the enumerated types of organizations classified as public charities as listed in IRS Publication 557. This list is set forth herein in Appendix B. Typical public charities include churches, educational organizations and hospitals. A corporation not falling within one of the categories listed in IRS Publication 557 may still avoid classification as a private foundation if it qualifies as a "publicly supported" organization or a "supporting organization." To qualify as either type of organization, certain specific tests must be met. These very detailed tests are beyond the scope of this Guidebook. A more complete discussion can be found in IRS Publication 557.

b. Restrictions And Taxes On Private Foundations

Private foundations generally are subject to a two percent excise tax on their net investment income (including capital gains). Private foundations are also subject to several other restrictions that may result in various taxes and penalties, including:

- restrictions on self-dealing between private foundations and their substantial contributors and other individuals described as "disqualified persons," including their directors and trustees;

- minimum requirements for distribution of income and principal for charitable purposes, as described below; and

- a potential tax upon termination of private foundation status.

a. **Self-Dealing Rules**

The prohibitions on self-dealing reach a broad range of transactions between a private foundation and a "disqualified person," including:

- the sale, exchange or leasing of property;

- the lending of money or other extensions of credit;

- the furnishing of goods, services or facilities;

- the payment of unreasonable compensation or expenses;

- the transfer to, or use by or for the benefit of, a disqualified person of the private foundation's income or assets; and

- payments to government officials.

In determining whether a transaction is restricted or prohibited by the self-dealing rules, it does not matter whether the transaction results in a benefit or a detriment to the private foundation or whether the transaction is "fair." The Code does, however, permit certain exceptions to the self-dealing rules, including, for example, the payment of reasonable compensation. Any transaction between a private foundation and a disqualified person should be reviewed by counsel or an appropriate committee to assure the self-dealing rules are not violated. Violations of the self-dealing restrictions may result in severe penalties and substantial legal complications.

VI TAXATION

b. Distribution Requirements

A private foundation must distribute annually a minimum amount for charitable purposes, which is roughly 5% of investment assets. The required distribution may take the form of a direct payment for charitable purposes, such as payment of expenses incurred in conducting a charitable activity, an acquisition of assets to be used in performing the organization's exempt purposes, or a contribution to another charitable organization.

If a private foundation satisfies its distribution requirements by making charitable contributions to other § 501(c)(3) exempt organizations, the foundation's responsibilities may not end at the time the contribution is made. Except where the contribution is made to a public charity or to certain operating foundations, the private foundation must take steps to assure that the contribution is, in fact, subsequently used by the receiving organization to accomplish exempt purposes. Some organizations, in very limited circumstances, may avoid this requirement.

c. Limitation On Excess Business Holdings

The Code imposes limitations on the ability of a private foundation to hold an ownership interest in another business entity, such as a corporation or a partnership.

d. Liability Of Foundation Managers

Excise taxes generally are imposed against a private foundation which violates any of the private foundation rules. In some cases, moreover, excise taxes may be imposed against "foundation managers," substantial contributors to the foundations, and, with respect to self-dealing, other "disqualified persons." Foundation managers include officers, directors, or trustees of a private foundation, and employees of the foundation who have authority or responsibility over the matter resulting in the tax.

VI TAXATION

4. § 501(c)(4) Organizations — Civic Leagues And Social Welfare Organizations

A nonprofit corporation operated exclusively for the promotion of social welfare may seek exemption under § 501(c)(4).

Exemption under this Section will not confer deductibility of contributions by donors to the corporation, but may enable it to avoid the restrictions of private foundation status, and the restrictions on lobbying and other political activity.

A nonprofit corporation which is operated exclusively for the promotion of social welfare may qualify as a § 501(c)(4) organization and thus be exempt from federal income tax.

a. Definition of Social Welfare

A corporation is operated exclusively for the promotion of social welfare if it is operated primarily to further the common good and general welfare of the people of a community, such as by bringing about civic betterment and social improvement. In addition, a § 501(c)(4) corporation must benefit a community as a whole. Thus, a corporation will not qualify under § 501(c)(4) if its activities benefit only its membership or a select group of individuals. Examples of the types of organizations that may qualify for § 501(c)(4) status are civic associations and volunteer fire companies or organizations engaged in crime prevention, etc.

A § 501(c)(4) corporation may not, as its primary activity, conduct a business with the general public in a commercial manner. Any earnings of such an organization must be devoted exclusively to charitable, educational, or recreational purposes.

b. Comparison Of § 501(c)(3) And § 501(c)(4)

Although the requirements for § 501(c)(3) and § 501(c)(4) appear to be similar, a corporation may more easily satisfy the requirements of § 501(c)(4). First, it may benefit a smaller or more specific group or community than would qualify a corporation for charitable status under § 501(c)(3). Second, a § 501(c)(4) organization may engage in some social activities, some lobbying, and some political activity.

§ 501(c)(3) status is preferable to § 501(c)(4) status if tax-deductible contributions or tax-exempt financing is important to the organization. However, § 501(c)(4) status may be advantageous if:

- lobbying will be a substantial part of the corporation's activities; or

- freedom to support or oppose candidates for office is sought;

- the organization would be subject to the restrictions imposed on a private foundation (as discussed above) if the organization were exempt under § 501(c)(3);

However, if an organization was once exempt as a § 501(c)(3) organization, but has lost its exemption because of lobbying or political campaign activities, it cannot then convert into a § 501(c)(4) organization.[8]

5. § 501(c)(6) Organizations

Nonprofit business leagues, chambers of commerce, trade associations, boards of trade and professional football leagues may qualify as § 501(c)(6) organizations.

a. Requirements For Exemption

A § 501(c)(6) corporation is an association of persons having a common business interest, the purpose of which is to promote such interest. These corporations must improve the business condition of the industry in general rather than benefitting individual members by supplying such members with such things as management services or improving the economy and convenience of conducting individual businesses. The corporation may satisfy this requirement if, as a whole, it represents all components of an industry or line of business within a particular geographic area. The corporation generally may not, however, be in competition with another group within the same industry or line of business, although members within the corporation may compete with each other.

There are certain examples of common activities worth noting that may affect a corporation's compliance with § 501(c)(6). On one hand, activities such as conducting an advertising campaign to promote an industry (rather than particular individuals) and publishing a trade publication for the benefit of an industry generally are considered activities that promote a particular line of business. On the other hand, activities such as operating a real estate multiple listing service and supplying management services and supplies to members have been found to benefit the members individually, rather than promote the industry or line of business as a whole. A § 501(c)(6) may engage in some business activities that do not promote an industry or line of business, subject to the rules relating to Unrelated Business Income discussed below, so long as such activities are not substantial.

b.   Tax Treatment Of Contributions Or Dues to a § 501(c)(6) corporation

As a general rule, contributions or dues payable to a § 501(c)(6) organization may be deductible as trade or business expenses except to the extent they are used to (1) participate in a political campaign on behalf of any candidate for public office; (2) engage in certain types of lobbying, or (3) attempt to influence legislation that is not of direct interest to the taxpayer's business. It should be noted, however that § 501(c)(6) contributions cannot be deducted as charitable contributions.

6.   Obtaining Tax-Exempt Status

With few exceptions, most § 501(c)(3) corporations must obtain IRS recognition of tax-exempt status and they hold such status only when and if such recognition is applicable. Other tax-exempt organizations should consider obtaining IRS recognition to ensure their tax-exempt status, but are not required to do so.

If a corporation is, in fact, organized and operated in accordance with the applicable requirements, the corporation may claim tax-exempt status without the need for an IRS ruling to that effect, unless exemption under § 501(c)(3) is sought. § 501(c)(3) corporations generally are required to obtain recognition of their tax-exempt status by the IRS as a condition to the tax exemption. § 501(c)(3) corporations that are not subject to the application requirement are (1) churches and certain other church-related corporations, and (2) corporations (other than private foundations) normally having annual gross receipts of not more than $5,000. In addition, certain corporations do not have to apply directly to the IRS for recognition of exemption under § 501(c)(3), because they are covered by a group exemption letter issued to a central organization. Other corporations should consider obtaining IRS recognition to ensure their tax-exempt status.

VI TAXATION

7. Unrelated Business Income

Any exempt corporation may be subject to a tax on Unrelated Business Income, if it regularly carries on a trade or business that is "unrelated" to its exempt purpose. If its unrelated business activities are more than insubstantial, the corporation may lose its tax exemption.

The Code permits an exempt organization to engage in some activities that are not related to its exempt purposes. Such activities are permissible so long as the exempt corporation's unrelated activities remain insubstantial when compared to the corporation's exempt activities.

The Code imposes a tax on certain income generated from the conduct of an "unrelated trade or business," in contrast to passive investment income, such as rents, dividends and interest. If the corporation has significant unrelated activities, a director should have a basic understanding of the types of activities that produce Unrelated Business Taxable Income (UBTI) to assure that the organization's unrelated business activities do not become substantial and that procedures are in place to monitor and properly report such activities to the IRS.

a.   Definition Of Unrelated Trade Or Business

An "unrelated trade or business" is any trade or business that is regularly carried on, the conduct of which is not substantially related to the corporation's exempt purposes. For example, the corporation may operate a store, or sell advertising in its publications.

An activity is "regularly carried on" if the activity is conducted with the frequency and continuity comparable to commercial activities of for-profit ventures.

An activity is "substantially related" (i.e., not "unrelated") to the corporation's exempt purposes if the activity contributes to the accomplishment of the corporation's exempt purposes other than through the production of income. The need for the funds generated by the activity does not make it "substantially related."

The Code excludes several types of activities from the definition of "unrelated trade or business." An activity will not be treated as an unrelated trade or business if:

- substantially all of the work is performed by volunteers;

- it is carried on primarily for the benefit of members, students, patients, officers, or employees;

- it consists of selling merchandise, substantially all of which has been donated;

- it relates to the distribution of low-cost articles ($5.00, indexed for inflation) in connection with charitable solicitations; or

- the business consists of a legal bingo game, in a State where bingo games are ordinarily not conducted on a commercial basis.

b.   Types of Income Excluded From UBTI

The Code excludes the following types of <u>income</u> from UBTI unless such income is "debt-financed."[9]

- dividends, interest, payments with respect to securities loans and annuities;

- royalties;

- most rents from real property;

- insubstantial rents from personal property when leased with real property;

- gain from the sale of capital assets; and

- certain research income.

c.   Use Of A Taxable Subsidiary

As noted above, an exempt corporation may conduct an insubstantial amount of unrelated activities itself. It is not necessary to establish a separate taxable corporation for such activities. However, an exempt corporation may choose to create a taxable subsidiary through which to conduct unrelated activities, especially if such activities would otherwise become substantial and thereby jeopardize the corporation's exempt status, or for non-tax reasons, such as the desire to limit the corporation's liabilities.

VI TAXATION

If a taxable subsidiary is formed, the subsidiary itself will be taxed on the income from the activities, but dividends paid by the taxable subsidiary to the exempt parent generally will not be UBTI.

The use of a taxable subsidiary requires careful tax planning as, in general, decisions made in the process are usually irrevocable. Future transfers of property from the taxable subsidiary to the exempt corporation and the eventual liquidation of the subsidiary may result in certain adverse tax consequences.

8. Special Reporting Requirements

a. Non-Charitable Contributions

The director must understand that exemption from federal income tax does not necessarily mean that donations to the corporation are deductible as charitable contributions and, if deductibility is not available, the corporation must disclose this fact.

Any tax-exempt corporation or political organization that is not eligible to receive charitable contributions—i.e. any corporation other than a § 501(c)(3) corporation—is required to disclose to its donors "in a conspicuous and easily recognizable format" in all fundraising solicitations, whether in written or printed form, by television or radio, or by telephone, that contributions to it are not deductible as charitable contributions for federal income tax purposes.[10]

b. Charitable Contributions In Return For Items Of Value

If a donor receives an item of value in return for a contribution to a § 501(c)(3) corporation, the Code requires that the donor's deduction be limited to the difference between the amount contributed and the fair market value of the goods or services received by the donor. For example, if a donor contributes $100 and receives a ticket to a symphony concert or a dinner that would normally cost $60, the donor is entitled to deduct $40.

The IRS has indicated its belief that in these situations § 501(c)(3) corporations have an obligation to inform their donors that the full amount of the contribution is not deductible and to indicate the fair market value of the goods or services received. Although no penalties are currently imposed for failure to make this disclosure, proper corporate practice, as currently followed by most organizations, is to indicate the amount of the contribution that is not deductible.[11]

c. Disclosure Of Annual Returns And Exemption Applications

Both annual information returns and IRS exemption applications must be made available by the tax-exempt organizations for public inspection.

Tax-exempt corporation must make their annual tax information returns and their IRS exemption applications, and related documentation and correspondence, available for public inspection at their principal offices and at all regional offices. The corporation may, however, withhold the names and addresses of its contributors and may also withhold any information relating to trade secrets, patents, processes, or styles of work, if the IRS determines that public disclosure of such information would adversely affect the organization.

A private foundation also must publish a notice in a newspaper of general circulation in the county in which the corporation's principal office is located stating that the corporation's annual return is available for inspection.

Corporation personnel who have a duty to comply with the public inspection requirements and fail to comply may be subject to penalties. Criminal penalties may be imposed on any person who willfully and knowingly furnishes false or fraudulent information.

VI TAXATION

SUGGESTED QUESTIONS CONCERNING TAXATION

1.   Is the corporation, on whose board I serve, exempt from federal income taxation?

2.   If it is, under what section of the Code is it exempt?

3.   If it is exempt under § 501(c)(3), is it a private foundation?

4.   If it is a private foundation, do I understand the special limitations that status imposes? Does the board and staff understand them?

5.   If we aren't exempt under § 501(c)(3), do we make clear to our donors that they cannot deduct their contributions to us?

6.   Who prepares our tax returns?

7.   What were the corporation's activities and mission as described to the IRS in applying for an exemption ruling? Is this description still an accurate portrayal of what we do?

8.   Do I know how much legislative activity we have engaged in? How much are we allowed under our particular exemption?

9.   What activities, if any, of our corporation may result in Unrelated Business Taxable Income?

10.   Who on our staff monitors this matter? Do our independent accountants do so?

11.   Do we make informational tax returns (IRS Form 990) available for public inspection? Does our office staff know of this obligation? If we are a private foundation, have we published the required notice stating where our annual return may be inspected?

THE NONPROFIT CORPORATION'S CHECKLIST: CHAPTER VI

Note: For purposes of simplicity in these checklists, we describe a corporation with a Chair, who presides over the Board of Directors; a Chief Executive, who may be a staff person; an Executive Committee; a Nominating Committee; and an Audit Committee. We also assume a Legal Counsel—someone, paid or unpaid, having primary responsibility for the Corporation's legal affairs. Many corporations have other Committees established for specific purposes, such as reviewing staff performance, fixing compensation, monitoring compliance with legal requirements and periodic review of bylaws. In many corporations the Executive Committee performs most or all of the functions, and these checklists will so assume.

SUBJECT	TO BE REVIEWED BY WHOM	HOW OFTEN	COMMENT
Federal Tax Questions			
1. If our corporation is exempt from federal income tax, under what section of the Internal Revenue Code is it exempt?	Legal Counsel	Annually	Whole board should understand basic nature of the corporation's specific exemption. Information on this subject should be in the director's manual.
2. If it is exempt under Section 501(c)(3), is the corporation a private foundation, a private operating foundation, or a public charity?	Legal Counsel, then full Board	Annually	Board should understand the privileges or limitations imposed by the applicable provisions of Code on the corporation's particular type of activity.

THE NONPROFIT CORPORATION'S CHECKLIST: CHAPTER VI

	SUBJECT	TO BE REVIEWED BY WHOM	HOW OFTEN	COMMENT
3.	If the corporation is exempt under Section 501(c)(3), have we engaged in activities which may be limited (in the case of lobbying) or prohibited (in the case of participating in an election)?	Legal Counsel, then full Board	Annually, and during discussion of any major change in contemplated political activities.	This is a field of tax law with frequent new interpretations. 501(c)(3) organizations should closely monitor activities to assure compliance.
4.	If the political activities of the corporation are restricted but not prohibited (as in the case of lobbying), have we compared the actual activities undertaken with the restrictions of applicable tax law?	Chief Executive, Legal Counsel	Annually	If such activities are substantial and continuing, the corporation's books should be organized to quantify such activities.

ENDNOTES

1. (p. 74) Our discussion, even of these limited areas, is based upon the law as it stood upon the date of this publication. The Internal Revenue Code is usually amended in some manner with each session of Congress, so some statements contained herein may be incomplete or inaccurate when they meet the reader's eyes. Nonetheless, the issues addressed are relatively permanent, and are areas requiring a director's attention.

2. (p. 74) Although many states rely on federal tax-exempt status in determining exemption from state income tax, some require separate filings. In addition, the requirements for exemption from real property and sales taxes typically may be more stringent. Generally, only certain § 501(c)(3) organizations (and usually not all of them) will qualify for such exemptions but the criteria vary from state to state.

3. (p. 74) Three significant types of tax-exempt organizations not included on Appendix B are: trusts held under qualified pension plans, state and local government instrumentalities, and political organizations. § 501(a) of the Code recognizes thirty-six categories of tax-exempt organizations, but the list includes some entities which are not corporations and hence are outside our concern.

4. (p. 75) An organization also may qualify under § 501(c)(3) if it is organized for testing for public safety; fostering national or international amateur sports competition (if no part of its activities involve providing athletic facilities or equipment); or preventing cruelty to children or animals. These specific exemptions are self-describing.

5. (p. 75) The limits on deductibility imposed by § 170(b) range from 20% to 50% of an individual contributor's income. A discussion of these limits is outside the scope of this Guidebook. See, however, IRS Publication 526, Charitable Contributions.

6. (p. 75) These requirements are set forth in detail in IRS Publication 557.

7. (p. 77) In this area, despite the reluctance of most government officials to challenge actions of religious organizations, the IRS has not hesitated: e.g., the settlement reached with Jimmy Swaggart Ministries arising from the endorsement, by that religious organization, of Pat Robertson's 1988 presidential candidacy. As part of this settlement of December 27, 1991, the organization paid over $170,000 in taxes and interest, and agreed to an extensive reorganization.

8. (p. 82) Code § 504(a) (1990).

9.   (p. 85) Code § 514 provides a special exception for real property acquired by certain "qualified organizations", including educational institutions and pension trusts. However, interest, rents, royalties and annuities paid by controlled for-profit subsidiaries to their exempt parent generally will not be excludable from income. To the extent that income is excluded from UBTI, any related deductions also are excluded from the computation of tax.

10.   (p. 86) Code § 6113. The rule does not apply to (a) organizations with annual gross receipts of $100,000 or less, or (b) any letter or telephone call if the communication is not part of a coordinated campaign soliciting more than 10 persons during the calendar year.

11.   (p. 86) IRS Publication 1391 provides a good summary of the IRS position on this issue.

VII

VOLUNTEERS AND ADVISORY BOARDS

Many nonprofit corporations find it useful to obtain the services of volunteers, advisory boards and other personnel who are neither directors nor officers of the corporation. The nonprofit director should understand the advantages and limitations of such devices.

Most public benefit and religious corporations and even many mutual benefit corporations find it either useful or, in some cases, necessary to create a volunteer program. For some similar reasons, many organizations seek to bring within the corporate activities special boards, committees or councils composed of persons not serving as directors but publicly identified with the corporation and its mission. This chapter will outline some considerations which the nonprofit director should bear in mind with regard to these activities.

1. Volunteers

The use of volunteers is generally confined to the public benefit or religious corporation, and, for many of them, it is a practice stemming from two needs: first of all, simply to obtain services that do not have to be paid for; and secondly, to motivate and identify individuals with the mission of the corporation.

The corporation, to begin with, will probably recognize that extensive use of volunteers inevitably requires devotion of some part of staff time and inevitably some part of the budget for their administration. Few volunteer programs can be administered well by volunteers.

Because of the problems involved in the use of volunteers, it is desirable that they be part of a program rather than enlisted on a random or sporadic basis. This does not mean that there is a need for having a large number of men and women so engaged, but it does mean that the decision is not haphazard or random. The board should consider the possible problems of staff morale and management authority involved in bringing in persons whose relationships can create tension.

Volunteers are agents of the corporation in the eyes of the law. That is to say, their acts or omissions, their care or negligence in their activities are, within limits, the acts or omissions of the corporation. The corporation, as a general rule, will not be exonerated from liability arising from the negligence of the agent simply because the agent was uncompensated or a volunteer.

There are exceptions to the foregoing statement and a number of statutory provisions in various states seek to insulate the corporation from liability arising from activities of an uncompensated person. However, nearly all such statutes still maintain that the corporation is liable for willful and wanton or malicious negligent acts of the person and such exceptions mean, as a practical matter, that the corporation cannot obtain dismissal in a lawsuit simply by proving that the person was uncompensated.

The board should make sure that the activities of volunteers are covered by the insurance program of the corporation. For example, if a public benefit corporation is engaged in the distribution of goods or services to some disadvantaged group, using the automobiles of a volunteer and with a volunteer driver, the corporation may be liable for injuries arising from negligent driving of that automobile, even though the corporation did not own the automobile or pay the driver. The corporation should also examine whether it can, or should, include volunteers within any provision for indemnification for liability imposed upon them, as previously discussed in this Guidebook. It is these difficulties that lead many corporations to avoid the use of voluntary help since it appears to expose the corporation to all the risks of fully employed personnel without the control and discipline involved in a paid staff.

The corporation, to minimize its exposure from such risk, should provide any volunteer with clear directions as to the scope of his or her activities and the purpose of the voluntary engagement. A memorandum setting forth such matters will, at the very least, record the corporate intent.

Lastly, there may be situations in which an individual does not serve as a full volunteer in the uncompensated sense but is employed by the corporation on a salary at substantially less than the market price for such services. The problems of employing such personnel may be principally management problems (e.g., the effect on the morale of other employees and the status accorded such a person), but otherwise the person should be treated as an employee for all purposes, particularly for purposes of insurance.

2. Advisory Bodies

A frequent device used in a nonprofit corporation, particularly in the public benefit field, is to appoint one or more auxiliary boards of directors, advisory committees, boards of sponsors, and the like.

Such devices may be useful in enabling a board to enlist the interest and activity of individuals who would be too numerous to serve on the board directly or who may not have time. Frequently public benefit corporations seek the endorsement of community leaders whose names will aid it in fundraising or political arenas, but who are unwilling to give the time commitments necessary for board service.

VII VOLUNTEERS AND ADVISORY BOARDS

The need for such groups will be generally self-evident. A board should, however, be aware of some problems which can exist in their creation and maintenance.

First of all, corporate law, in general, does not give an advisory board any particular status: it is not a body within the general pattern of duties, responsibilities and powers which have been outlined in this Guidebook as applicable to the board of directors.

At the same time, any group or individual publicly acknowledged to be connected with the corporation in some manner can, in some circumstances, be an agent of the corporation, binding it in some circumstances; the public statements or actions of such a group or individual may, at least in terms of public relations, be attributed to the board of directors; and the composition of such a board may raise many of the problems of conflict of interest previously described in this Guidebook. None of these problems are insoluble, but they do call for scrutiny and attention.

Furthermore, as has often been pointed out, if one purports to seek advice from a body outside the corporation's regular structure, the advice does not necessarily have to be followed, but unless the corporation is to treat its advisors with contempt, the advice must, at least, be considered. In short, unlike the regular committees of the board whose efficient functioning may lessen the burdens of the board, an advisory committee can increase those burdens by placing on the board an obligation to review its recommendations.

Accordingly, the first decision to be reached by the board is to define the purposes of the committee and relate them to the parallel functions of the board of directors in the oversight of the corporation's activities. No board can, or should, appoint a parallel committee simply to offer floating advice at its whim from time to time. The committee is unlikely to accept such a role and, if it did attempt to perform it, it would be disruptive at the least.

Secondly, the role of the advisory committee and its relationship to the staff should be defined in the same documents and decisions that create it. All the concerns mentioned herein concerning the dangers of board-staff relationships, below the chief executive level, would apply doubly with an advisory committee. This is not to say that such a level of communication is improper. Indeed, an advisory committee may be especially useful in dealing with the somewhat complex aspect of a corporation's program calling for broader participation than the board itself can provide. But the board should be aware, particularly where the advisory committee relates to a successful and enlarging function, of the danger of the committee and its related staff pulling the subject activity out of the corporation. Such events are not uncommon in the public benefit field.

The resolution or other corporate action creating the committee should designate the criteria for membership therein, the term for which the committee members are appointed and the power of some officer, director or the board itself to remove members of the committee. In general, the members of an advisory committee do not figure in the allocation of rights and duties within corporate law. They have no vested right to serve, no immunity from removal and no right to renewal of appointment. The board should be careful, however, to make sure that no resolutions or communications imply the creation of such rights.

An advisory committee properly constituted should be protected by the corporation's commitments of indemnification, insurance, and the like as described herein.

VII VOLUNTEERS AND ADVISORY BOARDS

SUGGESTED QUESTIONS CONCERNING
VOLUNTEERS AND ADVISORY BOARDS

1.   Do I know which of the corporation's programs use volunteers?

2.   How were they recruited?

3.   Do I understand what functions they perform?

4.   Do their functions overlap those of the paid staff?

5.   Do we have an advisory board or counsel?

6.   Do I understand its functions?

7.   Have I met the Chair or any members of the advisory board?

8.   How were they chosen?

THE NONPROFIT CORPORATION'S CHECKLIST: CHAPTER VII

Note: For purposes of simplicity in these checklists, we describe a corporation with a Chair, who presides over the Board of Directors; a Chief Executive, who may be a staff person; an Executive Committee; a Nominating Committee; and an Audit Committee. We also assume a Legal Counsel—someone, paid or unpaid, having primary responsibility for the Corporation's legal affairs. Many corporations have other Committees established for specific purposes, such as reviewing staff performance, fixing compensation, monitoring compliance with legal requirements and periodic review of bylaws. In many corporations the Executive Committee performs most or all of the functions, and these checklists will so assume.

	SUBJECT	TO BE REVIEWED BY WHOM	HOW OFTEN	COMMENT
1.	Does our corporation have a volunteer program?	Chief Executive, Full Board	Annually, or at inception of new program	Volunteer programs should always be formally approved.
2.	Are its functions defined in the corporate resolutions?	Chief Executive, Full Board	Annually, or at inception of new program	Volunteer programs should always be formally approved.
3.	Who administers the program at staff level?	Chef Executive	As needed, but reviewed annually.	
4.	Are the volunteers covered by the corporation's insurance program?	Chief Executive, Legal Counsel	Annually	Directors must understand that the inclusion of volunteers is not automatic.
5.	Are they subject to indemnification under the corporation's resolutions and bylaws concerning indemnification?	Chief Executive, Legal Counsel	Annually	Directors must understand that the inclusion of volunteers is not automatic.

THE NONPROFIT CORPORATION'S CHECKLIST: CHAPTER VII

	SUBJECT	TO BE REVIEWED BY WHOM	HOW OFTEN	COMMENT
6.	Do volunteers perform functions giving rise to significant risk such as driving automobiles on the corporation's business?	Chief Executive, Legal Counsel	Annually	It may be prudent to examine volunteer's personal coverage.
7.	Does our corporation have any board, committee or other body operating outside the board of directors, advising as to a particular function of the corporation? Is there a board resolution or other document which defines the function of the entity in question?	Chair, Chief Executive, Full Board	Annually	The corporation should be sure that such committees, if created, are both instructed and heard.
8.	How does it report to the board of directors? Is this on a regular schedule? How does the board analyze the recommendations of the entity?	Chair, Chief Executive, Full Board	Annually	The corporation should be sure that such committees, if created, are both instructed and heard.

THE NONPROFIT CORPORATION'S CHECKLIST: CHAPTER VII

	SUBJECT	TO BE REVIEWED BY WHOM	HOW OFTEN	COMMENT
9.	Does the board give the entity a regular response to its recommendations? How does it know what the board's reaction is with regard to its report?	Chair, Chief Executive, Full Board	Annually	Unless advisors are to be treated with contempt, they must be listened to.
10.	Do the members of the entity serve for a defined term? Are they subject to removal by the board of directors? How are they chosen?	Chair, Chief Executive, Legal Counsel	Annually	Removal and termination should be determined at creation of entity.

VIII

DIRECTORS' MANUALS AND ORIENTATION

The Corporation should institute formal actions and procedures to assure that all directors have received (and continue to receive) the basic documents of the corporation; and new directors should be given specific orientation as to the corporation's history, structure and activities.

A threshold obligation of a director is to know and understand the purpose, function and goals of the nonprofit corporation the director is serving. Orientation is one way to acquaint a director with the inside workings of the corporation. Tours, meetings with staff and management and use of written materials such as publications aimed at nonprofit corporation directors are all valuable tools which can be used to give a director a sense of what the corporation is about.

Another tool which can be invaluable in assisting directors of nonprofit corporations in complying with their duties as directors is a manual or manuals containing important documents relating to the governance and operation of the corporation and other information which will keep the director apprised of the current state of the corporation. These may be simple loose-leaf binders, with a table of contents and a tab for each item. Use of such a binder makes updating the manual easy.

The board may wish to have two manuals: one containing material which a director should have with him or her at every board meeting; and a bulkier volume for the director's home or office. In the event that a two-manual system is chosen, we suggest that the board meeting material include items listed below as "basic documents."

1. **Basic Documents.** The basic director's manual should contain, at a minimum, the following basic documents:

a. A calendar of dates and events compiled for the year, listing board, committee and other significant meetings, activities and deadlines, which can be updated periodically;

b. A copy of the corporation's articles of incorporation, and any amendments to such articles;

c. A copy of the current bylaws of the corporation;

d. A copy of the corporate mission statement;

e. A listing of names, addresses and phone numbers of the directors and officers of the corporation;

f.   A list of the corporation's committees, including the name of each committee chair and all committee members; and

g.   A list of staff members of the corporation, including positions, addresses and phone numbers.

2.   **Additional Material.** The following material, probably too bulky to be included in anything taken regularly to board meetings, but suitable for a director's personal use would be:

a.   Minutes of Board and Committee meetings, which can be retained in the manual for a year and then disposed of or filed elsewhere;

b.   Financial statements of the corporation for the prior fiscal year and the operating and capital budget for the current year;

c.   In the case of a multi-corporate structure, an organization chart setting forth the relationship of the corporation to any parent, subsidiary or affiliated corporations.

d.   Biographical data on directors and staff;

e.   A summary of D&O insurance, indemnification provisions available, and statutory exonerations;

f.   Current news releases;

g.   Annual Reports for the past two or three years;

h.   Conflict of interest policies; and

i.   Long range plan.

3.   **Information to the New Corporate Director.** When an individual is first elected to the board of directors (or is entertaining an invitation to be a nominee or to fill an existing vacancy on the board), there are several informational procedures which may be helpful to him or her.[1]

a.   **Corporate Records.** In particular, he or she should review the basic corporate documents listed above and consider major recent board actions by reviewing the minutes of the meetings of the board and its main committees for the last three years or so. In addition to determining the activities of the corporation and its methods of operation, this review also should be made to determine the stated purpose of the corporation as reflected in the articles and any mission statement of the organization. The individual also should examine the level of indemnification, and D&O insurance provided for directors, and whether limitations of liability are provided by state law and whether the corporation has complied with whatever is required for such limitation, either through provisions in its articles or bylaws, its policies, or by contract.

    b. **Financial Reports.** The prospective or new director should review the financial statements of the corporation for at least the last few years, noting particularly if there are any restrictions that have been placed on gifts to the corporation. He or she should consider reviewing IRS Form 1023 (Application for Recognition of Exemption) and any Forms 990 that have been filed with the IRS. If applicable, the official statement related to any recent bond financing also should be reviewed.

    c. **Current Directors.** The prospective or new director should be provided with the biographical data referred to above concerning all current and proposed directors.

    d. **Management Personnel.** Each such person should be provided with biographical data concerning the key executives of the corporation, and should have met the Chief Executive and other principal officers.

    e. **Compliance with Law and Internal Control.** As noted throughout this Guidebook the use of assets of a nonprofit corporation are subject to certain limitations. For example, they must be used for the purpose for which they are given, and they cannot inure to the benefit of a private individual. A prospective director should become familiar with the role of the corporation's accountants and legal advisors in regard to matters of internal control and legal compliance. She or he should learn the corporation's policies and procedures regarding conflict of interest. If the corporation does not have a public accountant or regular corporate counsel, the individual should determine what steps the corporation has taken to make sure it is in compliance with any applicable limitations. In addition, some nonprofit corporations are subject to being accredited or licensed by outside agencies. Review of accrediting or survey reports, if available, can be most helpful in determining problem areas needing attention.

    f. **Outlook.** The individual may find it helpful to have an in-depth discussion with the Chief Executive and Chair about the corporation's current plans, current prospects, critical issues being or expected to be confronted, and long-range objectives.

VIII DIRECTORS' MANUALS AND ORIENTATION

4. Orientation Meetings and Board Retreats

The Board and Management should organize specific events or meetings to welcome the new director, and should consider periodic retreats for the entire board to make extended review of corporate activity.

Effective use of a new board member requires that she or he learn as much as possible about the organization, its mission, history and hopes, as soon as possible. Leaving the new arrival to find this knowledge amid a group, all, or at least some of whom will be strangers, in a series of meetings, is a slow and inefficient process, and one in which many a promising board member is lost to a corporation.

We have outlined above the type of reading material the new board member might receive; we now suggest that this manual of resources be supplemented by and expanded through specific meetings with senior staff and the officers, at which corporate activities can be discussed in depth.

Somewhat the same considerations suggest a periodic board retreat: an extended board meeting dealing with larger issues of mission and the future; or discussing particular problems in depth the types of material which frequently are lost in a regular meeting's agenda. Such retreats are ineffective unless all, or a very high proportion of the board can attend, so they need to be scheduled long in advance, and are possibly infrequent events. But they should be considered by any nonprofit corporation with a general mission of significant size.[2]

VIII DIRECTORS' MANUALS AND ORIENTATION

SUGGESTED QUESTIONS CONCERNING
DIRECTORS' MANUALS AND ORIENTATION

1.   Do we have a regular manual containing the basic documents of the corporation?

2.   What documents does it contain?

3.   Does it include a memorandum on D&O insurance coverage?

4.   How do I keep it up to date?

5.   What files do I keep concerning my service as a director?

6.   Have we had a meeting or retreat reviewing the corporation's overall policies and mission or specific problems?

7.   Do I know of practices of other corporations concerning director orientation and training which our corporation could adopt?

THE NONPROFIT CORPORATION'S CHECKLIST: CHAPTER VIII

Note: For purposes of simplicity in these checklists, we describe a corporation with a Chair, who presides over the Board of Directors; a Chief Executive, who may be a staff person; an Executive Committee; a Nominating Committee; and an Audit Committee. We also assume a Legal Counsel—someone, paid or unpaid, having primary responsibility for the Corporation's legal affairs. Many corporations have other Committees established for specific purposes, such as reviewing staff performance, fixing compensation, monitoring compliance with legal requirements and periodic review of bylaws. In many corporations the Executive Committee performs most or all of the functions, and these checklists will so assume.

	SUBJECT	TO BE REVIEWED BY WHOM	HOW OFTEN	COMMENT
A.	Director's Manual	Chair, Chief Executive	At least annually, and in preparation for each meeting at which directors are elected.	A specific committee to undertake this task is recommended.
B.	Orientation	Chair, Chief Executive, Nominating Committee	At least annually, and in preparation for each meeting at which directors are elected.	A successful orientation meeting will take extensive time in planning and arranging for both board and staff participation.

ENDNOTES

1. (p. 102) A publication of the National Center for Nonprofit Boards may be helpful here: Nelson, <u>Six Keys to Recruiting, Orienting and Involving Nonprofit Board Members</u> (1991).

2. (p. 104) A good outline is contained in Bader, <u>Planning Successful Board Retreats</u> (National Center for Nonprofit Boards, 1991).

APPENDICES

APPENDIX A

The following is the Statement of Policy Governing Conflicts, in force at The Art Institute of Chicago. It is reproduced with the Institute's permission.

MEMBERS OF THE BOARD OF TRUSTEES AND STANDING AND ADVISORY COMMITTEES

GENERAL POLICY

Members of the Board of Trustees, members of Standing and Advisory Committees and members of the Women's Board and Auxiliary Board of The Art Institute of Chicago (the "Institute") must conduct their personal affairs in such a manner as to avoid any possible conflict of interest with their duties and responsibilities as members of The Art Institute of Chicago organization.

As to the Trustees, the Bylaws were amended in 1977 to provide as follows:

> Article VIII
>
> Any duality on the part of any Trustee shall be disclosed to the Board of Trustees, and made a matter of record through an annual procedure and also when the interest becomes a matter of Trustee action.
>
> Any Trustee having a duality of interest shall not vote or use his personal influence on the matter, and he shall not be counted in determining the quorum for the meeting. The minutes of the meeting shall reflect that a disclosure was made, the abstention from voting and the quorum situation.
>
> Any new Trustee will be advised of this policy upon entering the duties of his office.

A like standard shall apply to members of all Standing and Advisory Committees and members of the Women's Board and the Auxiliary Board. All such policies shall also be applicable to any member of one's immediate family or any person acting on his or her behalf.

Trustees, Committee members, Women's Board and Auxiliary Board members will be required to attest annually to their familiarity with Institute policies in this regard and to provide information concerning any possible conflict of interest so that disclosure may, if necessary, be made.

Whenever there exists a conflict the matter in question shall be made public by disclosure in the Annual Report unless otherwise directed by the Trustees.

SPECIFIC APPLICATION OF GENERAL POLICY

1.   Financial Interests:

"Financial interest" for this purpose shall mean any position as owner, officer, board member, partner, employee or other beneficiary. A possible conflict of interest arises when a Trustee, Committee member, or member of the Women's Board or Auxiliary Board holds a financial interest in or will receive any personal benefit from a business firm furnishing services, materials or supplies to the Institute. Assuming that the amount of business done by the Institute with any publicly held company has virtually no effect on the total results of such a company, "financial interest" shall not include the ownership of shares in a publicly held corporation.

2.   Collecting:

A potential area of conflict arises when a Trustee, Committee member, or member of the Women's Board or Auxiliary Board collects objects of a type collected by the Art Institute. Therefore, no Trustee, Committee member, or member of the Women's Board or Auxiliary Board shall knowingly compete with the Institute in the acquisition of objects. In the matter of collecting, any time that a conflict arises between the needs of the Institute and a person identified above, those of the Institute must prevail.

3.   Use of Institute Services, Property or Facilities:

Another area of potential conflict involves the use of Institute services or facilities. When a Trustee, Committee member, or member of the Women's Board or Auxiliary Board seek staff assistance or the use of Institute property or facilities they should not expect that such assistance will be rendered to an extent greater than that available to a member of the general public in similar circumstances or with similar needs. To the extent that extraordinary assistance is provided, there should be a clear understanding of how this assistance will benefit the Institute.

4.   Privileged Information:

A Trustee, Committee member, or member of the Women's Board or Auxiliary Board must never use the information received while serving the Institute if the personal use of such information would be detrimental in any way to the Institute. Any actions that might impair the reputation of the Institute must also be avoided.

5.   Dealing:

Trustees and members of curatorial committees shall not deal in fine art i.e. they shall not buy and sell for profit on a regular basis, maintain a financial interest in any dealership or gallery other than a passive interest of 5% or less, or receive a commission or other compensation for facilitating purchases or sales of fine art. This policy shall apply to all new members elected after August 13, 1990, the date of adoption of this policy.

June 16, 1980

Amended August 13, 1990

THE ART INSTITUTE OF CHICAGO

CONFLICT OF INTEREST QUESTIONNAIRE

NAME _____

HOME ADDRESS _____

ASSOCIATION WITH ART INSTITUTE OF CHICAGO _____

_____

BUSINESS AND PROFESSIONAL ACTIVITIES IN WHICH YOU OR AN IMMEDIATE FAMILY MEMBER HOLD AS OWNER, OFFICER, BOARD MEMBER, PARTNER, EMPLOYEE OR OTHER BENEFICIARY POSITION AS OF JUNE 30, 1989.

Name of Business/Professional Organization(s)
With Which You Are Associated   **Position Held/By Whom**

_____   _____

_____   _____

_____   _____

BEFORE COMPLETING THIS QUESTIONNAIRE: This Questionnaire should be completed only after a careful reading of the Policy Statement concerning Possible Conflicts of Interest. Your response should cover the period July 1, 1988 (or the day you became associated with the Institute if subsequent to this date) through June 30, 1989.

MAIL TO: The Office of the Vice President for Administrative Affairs
                The Art Institute of Chicago
                Michigan Avenue at Adams Street
                Chicago, Illinois 60603

AFFIRMATION: I have read The Art Institute of Chicago Statement of Policy dated June 16, 1980. I understand its provisions and I hereby affirm that, during the period indicated above, I have not, to the best of my knowledge and belief, been in a position of possible conflict of interest, except as indicated below:

POLICY	IF NO EXCEPTIONS PLEASE CHECK

1.   **FINANCIAL INTERESTS**   No Exceptions (___)

Describe exceptions, if any: _____

_____

_____

_____

2.   **COLLECTING**   No Exceptions (___)

Describe exceptions, if any: _____

_____

3.   **USE OF INSTITUTE SERVICES,**
     PROPERTY & FACILITIES   No Exceptions (___)

Describe exceptions, if any: _____

_____

4.   **PRIVILEGED INFORMATION**   No Exceptions (___)

Describe exceptions, if any: _____

_____

DATE _____   SIGNATURE: _____

APPENDIX B

Organization Reference Chart from
<u>Tax-Exempt Status for Your Organization</u>
Internal Revenue Service Publication 557 (Rev. Oct. 1988)

Section of 1986 Code	Description of organization	General nature of activities
501(c)(1)	Corporations Organized Under Act of Congress (including Federal Credit Unions)	Instrumentalities of the United States
501(c)(2)	Title Holding Corporation for Exempt Corporation	Holding title to property of an exempt organization
501(c)(3)	Religious, Educational, Charitable, Scientific, Literary, Testing for Public Safety, to Foster National or International Amateur Sports Competition, or Prevention of Cruelty to Children or Animals Organizations	Activities of nature implied by description of class of organization
501(c)(4)	Civic Leagues, Social Welfare Organizations, and Local Associations of Employees	Promotion of community welfare; charitable, educational or recreational
501(c)(5)	Labor, Agricultural, and Horticultural Organizations	Educational or instructive, the purpose being to improve conditions of work, and to improve products and efficiency
501(c)(6)	Business Leagues, Chambers of Commerce, Real Estate Boards, Etc.	Improvement of business conditions of one or more lines of business
501(c)(7)	Social and Recreation Clubs	Pleasure, recreation, social activities
501(c)(8)	Fraternal Beneficiary Societies and Associations	Lodge providing for payment of life, sickness, accident, or other benefits to members

501(c)(9)	Voluntary Employees' Beneficiary Associations	Providing for payment of life, sickness, accident or other benefits to members
501(c)(10)	Domestic Fraternal Societies and Associations	Lodge devoting its net earnings to charitable, fraternal, and other specified purposes. No life, sickness, or accident benefits to members
501(c)(11)	Teachers' Retirement Fund Associations	Teachers' association for payment of retirement benefits
501(c)(12)	Benevolent Life Insurance Associations, Mutual Ditch or Irrigation Companies, Mutual or Cooperative Telephone Companies, Etc.	Activities of a mutually beneficial nature similar to those implied by the description of class of organization
501(c)(13)	Cemetery Companies	Burials and incidental activities
501(c)(14)	State Chartered Credit Unions, Mutual Reserve Funds	Loans to members
501(c)(15)	Mutual Insurance Companies or Associations	Providing insurance to members substantially at cost
501(c)(16)	Cooperative Organizations to Finance Crop Operations	Financing crop operations in conjunction with activities of a marketing or purchasing association
501(c)(17)	Supplemental Unemployment Benefit Trusts	Provides for payment of supplemental unemployment compensation benefits
501(c)(18)	Employee Funded Pension Trust (created before June 25, 1959)	Payment of benefits under a pension plan funded by employees
501(c)(19)	Post or Organization of Past or Present Members of the Armed Forced	Activities implied by nature of organization
501(c)(21)	Black Lung Benefit Trusts	Funded by coal mine operators to satisfy their liability for disability or death due to black lung diseases

501(c)(22)	Withdrawal Liability Payment Fund	To provide funds to meet the liability of employers withdrawing from a multi-employer pension fund
501(c)(23)	Veterans Organization (created before 1880)	To provide insurance and other benefits to veterans
501(d)	Religious and Apostolic Associations	Regular business activities. Communal religious community
501(e)	Cooperative Hospital Service Organizations	Performs cooperative services for hospitals
501(f)	Cooperative Service Organizations of Operating Educational Organizations	Performs collective investment services for educational organizations
501(k)	Child Care Organization	Provides care for children
521(a)	Farmers' Cooperative Associations	Cooperative marketing and purchasing for agricultural producers

APPENDIX C

SUGGESTED READING

The general literature on nonprofit boards and corporations is becoming extensive and this Appendix does not purport to cover all titles, particularly in view of the uneven quality of some of the material currently offered on the market. The following, however, merit perhaps more extensive attention:

First and foremost is Michael Hone, Reporter, <u>Revised Model Nonprofit Corporation Act, Official Text with Official Comments and Statutory Cross-References</u> (Prentice Hall, Law and Business, Clifton, N.Y. 1988).

A general review of the function of the nonprofit board, addressed almost entirely to public benefit board, is Houle, <u>Governing Boards</u> (Jossey-Bass, Inc., San Francisco, California 94104, 1989).

Howe, <u>The Board Member's Guide to Fund Raising</u> (Jossey-Bass, 1991). This is a good general discussion of the subject matter described in the title. Again, it is a work largely dealing with the public benefit corporation.

Kurtz, <u>Board Liability</u> (Moyer, Bell, Mount Kisco, New York, 1988) is an excellent analysis of the role of the public benefit corporation director and extends beyond the comparatively narrow issue which the title implies.

Wolf, <u>Managing a Nonprofit Corporation</u> (Prentice Hall Press, New York, N.Y. 2d Ed. 1990) is a good general text for public benefit or community organization directors, although it suffers some from a frequent use of fictional illustrations of problems (which seems to be something of a habit of those writing in this field).

The American Society of Corporate Secretaries (1270 Avenue of the Americas, New York, N.Y. 10020) publishes a number of materials, mostly intended for the business corporation, but some of which are relevant here. The Society's <u>Meetings of the Board of Directors and Its Committees</u> (1985) is a detailed text.

Lastly, two specialist publications of high quality are Ullberg & Ullberg, <u>Museum Trusteeship</u> (American Association of Museums, Washington, D.C., 1981), and

Stanton, <u>Trustee Handbook</u> (National Association of Independent Schools, Boston, Massachusetts, 6th Ed., 1989).

A reader interested in pursuing further material in this area should consult the National Center for Nonprofit Boards, 1225 19th Street, N.W., Suite 340, Washington, D.C. 10036 which has an extended bibliography; and, among several publishers, Jossey-Bass, Inc., Publishers, 350 Sansome Street, San Francisco, California 94104.

In the End Notes throughout this guidebook, there are references to various texts on various topics. Each of these reflects a recommendation of relevance as to the particular subject involved

A recent issue of the Harvard Law Review presents a general examination of the nonprofit world. <u>Developments in the Law–Nonprofit Corporations,</u> 105 Harv. L. Rev. 1579 (1992).

NONPROFIT BOOKS FROM THE ABA

Guidebook for Directors of Nonprofit Corporations
(PC#: 5070264)

_____copies @ $19.95 each (1-4 copies)

_____copies @ $14.95 each (5-25 copies)

_____copies @ $12.95 each (26-100 copies)

_____copies @ $9.95 each (101+ copies)

Nonprofit Governance: The Executive's Guide
(PC#: 5070305)

_____copies @ $79.95 each (1-3 copies)

_____copies @ $59.95 each (4-10 copies)

_____copies @ $49.95 each (11-50 copies)

$_____Subtotal

$_____Tax (DC residents add 5.75%, IL residents add 8.75%, MD residents add 5%)

$_____Handling (orders up to $49.99 add $4.95, orders $50+ add $5.95)

$_____Total

PAYMENT:

☐ Bill me   ☐ Check enclosed payable to the ABA   ☐ VISA   ☐ MasterCard

Acct #_____ Exp.Date_____

Signature_____

Name_____

Firm/Org_____

Address_____

City/State/Zip_____

Phone number (in case we have a question about your order)_____

Mail to: ABA, Publication Orders, P.O. Box 10892, Chicago, IL 60610-0892

Or Phone: 1-800-285-2221

Or Fax: 312-988-5568

source code: BOOK